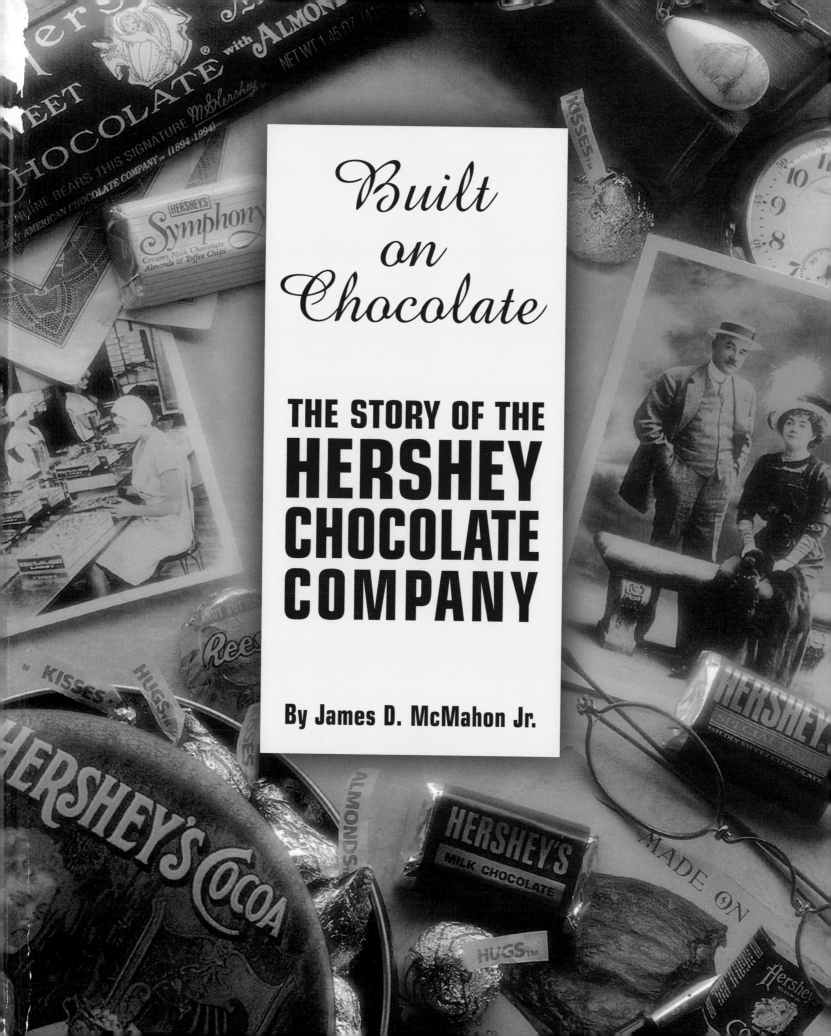

Built on Chocolate

THE STORY OF THE HERSHEY CHOCOLATE COMPANY

By James D. McMahon Jr.

View of Founders Hall, Milton Hershey School. Founders Hall on the campus of the Milton Hershey School was dedicated to the memory of Milton Hershey on September 13, 1970. It serves as the school's main administrative building and visitors center. The building provides meeting rooms, an auditorium, cafeteria, and various administrative and business offices.

Publisher: W. Quay Hays
Editorial Director: Peter L. Hoffman
Editor: Steve Baeck
Art Director: Chitra Sekhar
Photography: Stewart Sargent
Creative Direction: Dart Flipcards Inc.
Production Director: Trudihope Schlomowitz
Prepress Manager: Bill Castillo
Production Artists: Gaston Moraga and Bill Neary
Production Assistants: Tom Archibeque, David Chadderdon, and Russel Lockwood

For information:
General Publishing Group, Inc.
2701 Ocean Park Boulevard, Suite 140
Santa Monica, CA 90405

Library of Congress Cataloging-in-Publication Data

McMahon, James D., Jr.
    Built on Chocolate : the story of the Hershey
Chocolate Company / by James D. McMahon.
        p.   cm.
    Includes bibliographic references (p. 206).
    ISBN 1-57544-033-4 (hc)
    1. Hershey, Milton Snavely, 1857–1945. 2. Hershey
Chocolate Corporation--Biography. 3. Chocolate
industry--United States--History. 4. Businesspeople--
United States--Biography.   I. Title.
HD9200.U52H474   1998
338.7'6645--dc21   98-29196
                                                    CIP

Printed in the USA by Worzalla

10 9 8 7 6 5 4

General Publishing Group
Los Angeles

TABLE OF CONTENTS

THE AUTHOR WOULD LIKE TO EXPRESS HIS SINCERE THANKS AND APPRECIATION TO THE FOLLOWING FOR THEIR ASSISTANCE IN PREPARING AND REVIEWING THIS MANUSCRIPT FOR PUBLICATION:

THE STAFF OF THE HERSHEY MUSEUM

David L. Parke, Jr., Executive Director

Mary D. Houts, Associate Director/Senior Curator of Education

Amy L. Bischof, Curatorial Assistant

Jan M. Hester, Museum Shop Manager/Tour Coordinator

Lois I. Miklas, Curator of Education/Schools and Visitor Services

Tanya T. Richter, Curator of Education/Public Programs and Information

Sharon A. Smith, Assistant Office Manager/Volunteer Coordinator

Amy T. Taber, Public Relations Coordinator/Public Programs Assistant

Karen L. Yermalovich, Office Manager/Membership Coordinator

HERSHEY COMMUNITY ARCHIVES

Pamela C. Whitenack, Archivist

DART FLIPCARDS INC.

Stewart Sargent

GENERAL PUBLISHING GROUP

Steve Baeck

HERSHEY FOODS CORPORATION

Dawn Colon

TO MY DAUGHTER KATIE

WHO SHARED HER FATHER AND MANY OF HER WEEKENDS

IN HELPING TO MAKE THIS BOOK A REALITY

Introduction

Hershey: One Name, Many Stories

Hershey's. The very name has come to be synonymous with quality milk chocolate. Although the Hershey reputation is largely built on chocolate, many people are surprised to learn that the story of Hershey is more than the story of one man and the chocolate bar that bears his name. Hershey is also the name of a vibrant Central Pennsylvania community; the leading North American manufacturer of quality chocolate, confections, and pasta products; a state-of-the-art teaching hospital and medical center; a school for disadvantaged youth; several hotels, sports and entertainment attractions, commercial establishments, and philanthropic institutions designed to serve the public interest; and the man who created them all—Milton S. Hershey. The Hershey story, then, is the sum total of those people, places, and institutions who share in the Hershey name.

Built on Chocolate is an attempt to document the Hershey story in the broadest possible strokes using photographs, product packaging, advertising, archival records, memorabilia, personal remembrances, and related ephemera. It is in no way an attempt to chronicle the life of Mr. Hershey or the history of each of his many business and philanthropic endeavors. Indeed, such an effort would be extremely difficult to carry out today. Although he was 88 years old when he died in 1945, it is important to note that Mr. Hershey left almost no written record of himself. He kept no diaries and wrote no memoirs. It was not his habit to write letters. He and his wife had no children. Much of what is known about Mr. Hershey is derived from secondary sources or interviews with individuals many years after

the fact or long after his death. Often these recollections of business associates, competitors, employees, and even Mr. Hershey himself have contained unsubstantiated, embellished, or erroneous information. The ability to substantiate many of these stories is also hampered by the lack of early corporate business records. Many of the holes in our story may never be filled.

Since Mr. Hershey's death in 1945, the Hershey story has taken on near mythological proportions. Separating fact from fiction is often difficult—but not impossible. It is the mission of the Hershey Museum to accurately communicate the Hershey story to the public through the interpretation and use of its collections. Milton Hershey created the museum in 1933 as a resource for the Hershey community. Originally a museum of Native American cultural material, the collection has grown to include objects of Pennsylvania German decorative arts and everyday life as well as the largest publicly held collection of Hershey objects and related memorabilia. Much of the information and all of the objects in this book, unless otherwise noted, are from the permanent collections of the Hershey Museum and the Hershey Community Archives, educational services of the M.S. Hershey Foundation. "Built

The American Dream. The success of the Hershey Chocolate Company gave Milton Hershey the means to carry out his most important goals: building a model town to benefit his workers and starting the Milton Hershey School for disadvantaged children.

Hershey's Chocolate. In a little more than 100 years, the Hershey Chocolate Company has grown from a single plant in Lancaster, Pennsylvania, to a multinational corporation operating numerous manufacturing facilities. Among the company's major production facilities are those in Hershey, Pennsylvania; Oakdale, California; Stuarts Draft, Virginia; and Smith Falls, Ontario, Canada.

Milton Snavely Hershey 1857–1945. Milton Hershey was born in a farmhouse a mile from where he would eventually build his chocolate factory and the surrounding town that bears his name. His family moved often when he was young. He attended several schools, but only received a limited formal education. Apprenticed to a confectioner at a young age, he started his first candy business when he was only 18. Although he experienced numerous failures, he continued to work very hard and did not become successful until he was over 30 years old.

Hometown Favorites

on Chocolate" is the name of the museum's permanent Hershey exhibit and the inspiration for this book. Both efforts are indicative of the variety of interpretive avenues used by the museum to fulfill its mission.

The story of Hershey begins with the story of Milton S. Hershey—the Man Behind the Chocolate Bar—who made all of this possible. The story of Mr. Hershey's business fortunes continues to fascinate us today. His story is the very embodiment of the American Dream: the rise of a boy from modest beginnings who—by industry, thrift, perseverance, and a little luck—became a world-famous, wealthy, and respected entrepreneur and philanthropist. It has been my pleasure and good fortune to play a part in chronicling and documenting these stories during my tenure as Curator of Collections and Exhibitions for the Hershey Museum since 1988. I hope this book will impart some of that wonder, respect, and curiosity to you as well.

Chapter 1

If At First You Don't Succeed

Try, Try, Again

The Homestead circa 1910. This is the farmhouse built in 1826 by Milton Hershey's grandparents. Passed down to Henry Hershey by the time Milton was born here in 1857, it was sold to satisfy creditors in the mid-1860s. After achieving success in Lancaster, Milton Hershey repurchased the home in 1897. In 1909, it became the first location of his school for orphan boys.

A STRICT UPBRINGING

Milton Snavely Hershey was born September 13, 1857, the only surviving child of Henry and Veronica "Fanny" Snavely Hershey. He was born in a farmhouse in Derry Township, Dauphin County, Pennsylvania, only a few miles from the present site of the town of Hershey. Both parents shared a Mennonite heritage and were raised in households adhering to a strict lifestyle. The Mennonites are one of the better-known groups of Pennsylvania Germans or "Pennsylvania Dutch" who emigrated to South Central Pennsylvania in the 18th century from the German-speaking area of Central Europe known as the Palatinate, an area of mixed German, Swiss, and French ethnicity.

Henry Hershey, a tall handsome man, was noted for his alert and inquiring mind. Unfortunately, he lacked the perseverance needed to succeed in the multitude of projects and dreams he conceived. Fanny Hershey was a plain-dressing woman who adhered to the Reformed Mennonite Church values of thrift, hard work, and frugality. Although Milton Hershey never became a member of the Reformed Mennonites, he was strongly influenced by their values as exemplified by his mother and his father's brother, Bishop Elias Hershey. Milton Hershey was able to combine

Coverlet 1841. Typical of the professionally woven coverlets of the period, this example was woven by Christian Yordy of the town of Willow Street in Lancaster County for Elizabeth Snavely, Milton Hershey's maternal grandmother.

Henry Hershey circa 1900. Milton Hershey's father was never successful at making a living. His numerous failures and frequent journeys resulted in the breakdown of his marriage.

Veronica "Fanny" Snavely Hershey circa 1910. Mrs. Hershey, or "Mother" Hershey, wore the plain garb of the Reformed Mennonite Church throughout her life. She worked tirelessly for her son on behalf of his early business ventures and remained a cherished adviser throughout his life.

the best qualities of both of his parents: from his father a love of invention and adventure, from his mother a sense of industry and perseverance. The clash in personalities and temperament between Henry and Fanny Hershey led to an early estrangement between husband and wife that was never fully resolved. Despite the differences between his parents, Milton Hershey remained close to each of them throughout his life.

Many people are interested in the genealogy of the Hershey family. Some are intrigued by the Pennsylvania German and Mennonite background of the family. Others, more familiar with the name, are looking for a more personal connection. The Hershey surname is a very common last name in South Central Pennsylvania and it seems nearly everyone with a Hershey in his or her family wants to know if they are related to Milton Hershey. Those most familiar with the Hershey story look to the Hershey family for insights into the very personality of Milton Hershey himself. Both of Milton Hershey's parents are descended from Swiss Mennonite families. In German-speaking areas of Europe, the name traditionally appears as Hirschi or Hersche. Christian Hirschi, Mr. Hershey's direct ancestor, emigrated to America in 1717 as part of a large group of German-speaking immigrants, most of whom were Mennonites. He settled in Lancaster County,

Derry Church Schoolhouse circa 1925. This is the one-room schoolhouse where Milton Hershey attended second grade. Today, the structure is located next to High Point Mansion, the home built by Milton Hershey in 1908 in Hershey, Pennsylvania.

Pennsylvania, where he died in 1722. His son Bentz, or Benjamin (1696–1789), was a prominent Mennonite bishop who had a son named Christian (1719–1782). Christian's son Isaac (1773–1831) brought the Hershey family to Derry Township in Dauphin County. In 1826, he built the Homestead, the home where Milton Hershey was born, which is preserved today as part of the Milton Hershey School. Isaac's son Jacob Hershey (1802–1877) married a distant cousin, Nancy Hershey. They had a number of children who quickly grasped the opportunities the "modern" world had to offer, but with varying degrees of success.

The oldest and most restless of Jacob Hershey's children was Henry Hershey (1829–1904), the father of Milton Hershey. He seems to have suffered the most from the dichotomy between his father's times and his own. The other children seemed to make a go of life. Henry's younger brother, Joseph, became a physician; another brother, Elias, became a bishop in the Reformed Mennonite Church and a favorite of young Milton; a third brother, Christian, became a successful inventor and patent holder; a fourth brother, Jacob, remained on the land as a successful farmer. Henry Hershey married

Fanny B. Snavely (1835–1920) on January 15, 1856. Fanny's father was Bishop Abraham Snavely, a respected member of the Reformed Mennonite Church and a well-to-do man in his own right. She had a little of her own money, which the various ventures of her husband quickly exhausted. As time went on, she lost patience with her husband and, except for their common interest in their son, they quickly drifted apart. In addition to Milton (1857–

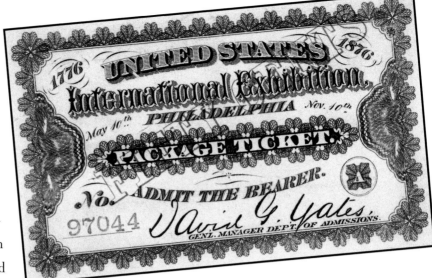

1945), a second child, Sarena was born in 1862, but she died five years later. In 1898, Milton married Catherine Sweeney (1872–1915). The marriage produced no children.

By all accounts Milton Hershey had quite an unsettled childhood. Henry's restlessness resulted in the family moving numerous times during the first 13 years of young Milton's life before finally ending up in the small village of Nine Points in southern Lancaster County. Milton received little formal education or continuity in his studies, which even his father's interests in books could not overcome. Indeed, his father was often away for long periods and his mother made little effort to correct the impression that they were separated or that her husband might be dead, a situation that might

Admission Ticket—Centennial International Exhibition.
Approximately one-quarter of the population of the United States traveled to Philadelphia in the summer of 1876 to visit the exposition held in honor of the nation's 100th birthday. Here Milton Hershey set out to make his mark upon the world, hoping to take advantage of the large crowds expected for the celebration.

help explain Milton's later interest in creating a school devoted to the education and welfare of orphaned boys.

In an effort to teach his son a trade in line with his own interests, Henry apprenticed his son to Samuel Ernst, a local printer who published a German–English language newspaper entitled *Der Waffenlose Waechter* (*The Weaponless Watchman*). Milton was ill-suited to the work and the experiment did not last long. Now completely fed up with Henry's wanderings and the effects of them on the welfare of her son, Fanny Hershey took control of Milton's education. The 14-year-old Milton Hershey was apprenticed to Joseph Royer, a successful confectioner in Lancaster City. During his four-year apprenticeship, Milton developed his natural flair for mixing ingredients. He learned that candy making was as much an art as a science and that he needed to rely on his innate abilities and talents in developing tasty confections. Fanny's devotion, as well as that of her sister, Martha "Mattie" Snavely, was now focused solely on Milton. For some years, the Snavely family would be his chief financiers and supporters.

MAKING HIS WAY

In 1876, 18-year-old Milton Hershey established his first candy-making business in Philadelphia. He hoped to find a ready market for his candy in the Centennial Exposition crowds. A celebration of America's achievements during its first 100 years,

Trade Card 1876–1879.
On June 1, 1876, Milton Hershey set up business for himself in Philadelphia. With an eye to the Centennial market, he printed a business card picturing the Exhibition's Machinery Hall. He was 18 years old. His assets consisted chiefly of $150 borrowed from his aunt, Martha Snavely. For his first three years in Philadelphia, Hershey established himself at 935 Spring Garden Street. It was a small place, but he could not afford better.

This is the storefront on Spring Garden Street. The photograph was taken in the 1950s.

the Exposition opened in Fairmount Park in 1876. Despite hard work, long hours, and the support of his mother, her sister Aunt Mattie, and others (including his father who joined Milton in 1881–1882 for a short period), his business failed. His effort was hampered by small volume, an overly diverse product line, and little cash flow. In 1882, after six years of effort, Milton Hershey's first candy business failed. That same year, Hershey left Philadelphia to follow his father to Denver, Colorado, to try his luck in mining silver. When this failed, he took a job with a Denver candy maker. Here he learned the secret of making caramels with fresh milk. Milk improved their flavor and kept them fresh much longer than those of other makers who used inferior ingredients, including paraffin. Unable to find an opportunity to start his own candy business, Milton Hershey left Colorado after only a few months. He then worked for a short period making caramels for Wilbur F. Day, a candy maker in Morristown, New Jersey. In 1883, Milton Hershey traveled to New York City, the largest candy market in the world, to try again in the candy-making business. Despite a good product and tireless effort, he was not successful. In 1886, he left New York and returned to Lancaster penniless. He was now 29 years old.

THE FIRST MILLION IS THE HARDEST

Despite his two failures, Milton Hershey was ready to start again in Lancaster. Most of his family, always his staunchest supporters, now refused or were unable to assist him. Armed only with the support of his mother, Aunt Mattie, and William Henry Lebkicher, a Civil War veteran and a former Philadelphia employee, Milton Hershey began producing milk caramels soon after his arrival in Lancaster. The Lancaster milk caramel business, known as the Lancaster Caramel Company, began like the two earlier ventures. He didn't have the equipment, staff, or cash flow to produce enough penny goods to make a profit. To succeed he needed to expand his operation. The turning point came when a British candy importer offered to market Hershey's milk caramels abroad. Based on this order, Milton Hershey convinced a local bank to lend him the necessary capital he needed to purchase equipment and raw ingredients to produce large quantities of milk caramel candies.

Martha "Mattie" Snavely circa 1880. Milton Hershey's aunt helped with money and advice during his early years in business.

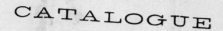

CATALOGUE

–AND–

PRICE-LIST

–OF–

EXHIBITING CASES AND CONFECTIONS

MANUFACTURED BY

MILTON S. HERSHEY,

Nos. 1217 TO 1225 BEACH STREET,

PHILADELPHIA.

A WORD TO THE TRADE.

In presenting this Circular to the business world, I take pleasure in recording the fact that my anticipations last season of specialties in my line have been amply realized, and the prospects for the coming season are uniformly bright.

There must always be ample business and good profit for all dealers in the Confectionery trade who have the wisdom to buy first-class goods, and by using none but the best material, and displaying it to the customers in the best style.

Notwithstanding the attention of Manufacturers, wholesalers especially, have been directed to many improvements in business, there is still room for economizing, by which the profits can be greatly increased, indeed none but a profitable business could sustain the rude and wasteful system generally prevailing in the trade.

The injuries done in the past years to the Confectionery business by the use of cheap material and adulteration is incalculable, and it is a most encouraging sign of the times that, considering only the direct folly of this course, the losses incurred are becoming more clearly seen every day. Among the new and thoroughly tested improvements lately introduced, I invite *special* attention to my *Candy Cabinet for Druggists and Grocers.* They form a very handsome counter ornament. They require no re-packing of goods and are ready for disposing of goods at once. A customer can thus see specimens of entire stock from which to make a selection, while the samples displayed are secured against handling, intrusion of dust, insects, etc.

A selection having been made, a supply corresponding to it can be obtained from the drawers, which being kept closed and being only accessible from behind the Cabinet are not liable to the intrusion, which renders a display of goods openly subject to so many objections on the part of the dealer, and renders them liable to many serious losses and inconveniences. The difficulty experienced by many in obtaining high grades of goods of uniform quality has been felt, as unscrupulous manufacturers of inferior goods have overrun the market at prices as low as even the cost of the material for the production of pure goods.

Thus many inferior goods are put on the public and sold for the best. During the past few years the undeniable superiority of my Cabinets and general stock has attracted very large patronage from first-class Druggists and Grocers, the trade demands the finest goods that can be produced.

DESCRIPTIVE CATALOGUE.

CABINET.

Height, 19 inches.   Depth, 13 inches.

MILTON S. HERSHEY PHILA

Width, 18 inches.
Patented March 15th, 1881.

These Cabinets are neat and of imposing appearance. Constructed of Walnut and Ash. The whole of superior workmanship, and are made to hold 60 lbs. of Candy.

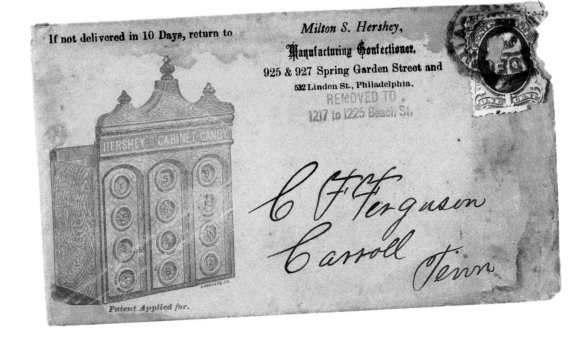

If not delivered in 10 Days, return to

Milton S. Hershey,
Manufacturing Confectioner,
925 & 927 Spring Garden Street and
532 Linden St., Philadelphia.

REMOVED TO
1217 to 1225 Beach St.

HERSHEY'S CABINET CANDY

Patent Applied for.

C. F. Ferguson
Carroll
Tenn.

Retail price of Cabinet, *Wood Drawers*,	$6.00
" " " *Tin Drawers*,	7.50
Cabinets filled with fine Confections, suitable for Grocers, 60 lbs., 12 varieties, *Wood Drawers*,	15.00
" " " " *Tin Drawers*,	17.00
Cabinets, suitable for Druggists, 60 lbs., 12 varieties, *Wood Drawers*,	18.00
" " " " *Tin Drawers*,	20.00
Cabinets filled with assorted Caramels, 100 lbs.	25.00

This cut represents an Exhibiting Case for retailing goods, very handy and the cheapness recommends it at once. It contains 30 lbs., 6 varieties of fine Candies. Sold at $6.00.

The following list of goods are packed in my 5 lb. Patent Display Box, as shown in the above cut, thus making a complete retailing case:

CARAMELS.

Vanilla, extra fine,	25c.
Chocolate,	"
Strawberry,	"
Raspberry,	"
Shellbark,	"
Cocoanut,	"
Maple,	"
Almond,	"
Walnut,	"
Orange,	"
Lemon,	"
Roman Punch.	"

CHOCOLATE GOODS.

Hand-made Cream Chocolates,	20c.
" Vanilla, No. 1,	25c.
" " Double,	40c.
" Orange,	25c.
" Spanish, Assorted,	25c.
" Coffee,	30c.
Choc. Nonpareils,	25c.
" Wafers,	35c.
Jelly Chocolates, No. 1,	45c.
Roast Almonds, (choc.) No. 1,	"
St. Nicholas,	"
Nougatinas,	"
Bramble,	"
Jim Crows,	"
Bon Bons.	"

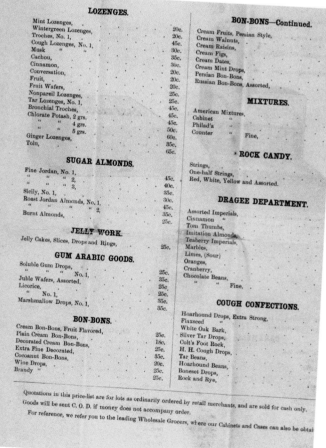

LOZENGES.

Mint Lozenges,	20c.
Wintergreen Lozenges,	20c.
Troches, No. 1,	45c.
Cough Lozenges, No. 1,	30c.
Musk	35c.
Cachou,	30c.
Cinnamon,	20c.
Conversation,	20c.
Fruit,	20c.
Fruit Wafers,	25c.
Nonpareil Lozenges,	25c.
Tar Lozenges, No. 1,	45c.
Bronchial Troches,	45c.
Chlorate Potash, 2 grs.	45c.
" " 4 grs.	50c.
" " 5 grs.	60c.
Ginger Lozenges,	35c.
Tolu,	65c.

SUGAR ALMONDS.

Fine Jordan, No. 1,	
" " No. 2,	45c.
" " No. 3,	40c.
Sicily, No. 1,	35c.
Roast Jordan Almonds, No. 1,	30c.
" " No. 2,	45c.
Burnt Almonds,	35c.
	25c.

JELLY WORK.

Jelly Cakes, Slices, Drops and Rings,	25c.

GUM ARABIC GOODS.

Soluble Gum Drops,	25c.
" " No. 1,	35c.
Juble Wafers, Assorted,	25c.
Licorice,	25c.
" No. 1,	35c.
Marshmallow Drops, No. 1,	35c.

BON-BONS.

Cream Bon-Bons, Fruit Flavored,	25c.
Plain Cream Bon-Bons,	18c.
Decorated Cream Bon-Bons,	25c.
Extra Fine Decorated,	35c.
Cocoanut Bon-Bons,	20c.
Wine Drops,	25c.
Brandy "	25c.

BON-BONS—Continued.

Cream Fruits, Persian Style,
Cream Walnuts,
Cream Raisins,
Cream Figs,
Cream Dates,
Cream Mint Drops,
Persian Bon-Bons,
Russian Bon-Bons, Assorted,

MIXTURES.

American Mixtures,
Cabinet   "
Philad'a   "
Counter   " Fine,

ROCK CANDY.

Strings,
One-half Strings,
Red, White, Yellow and Assorted.

DRAGEE DEPARTMENT.

Assorted Imperials,
Cinnamon   "
Tom Thumbs,
Imitation Almonds,
Teaberry Imperials,
Marbles,
Limes, (Sour)
Oranges,
Cranberry,
Chocolate Beans,
"   " Fine,

COUGH CONFECTIONS.

Hoarhound Drops, Extra Strong,
Flaxseed   "
White Oak Bark,
Silver Tar Drops,
Colt's Foot Rock,
H. H. Cough Drops,
Tar Beans,
Hoarhound Beans,
Boneset Drops,
Rock and Rye,

Quotations in this price-list are for lots as ordinarily ordered by retail merchants, and are sold for cash only.
Goods will be sent C. O. D. if money does not accompany order.
For reference, we refer you to the leading Wholesale Grocers, where our Cabinets and Cases can also be obtai[ned]

Business Envelope, Catalogue, and Price List circa 1881. After the return of Henry Hershey to his son's side in 1881, Milton Hershey moved his business to Beach Street in an effort to concentrate on the wholesale end of his business. According to his *Catalogue and Price-List*, "Quotations in this price list are for lots as ordinarily ordered by retail merchants, and are sold for cash only." The catalogue shows the variety of products he continued to manufacture, including caramels, chocolate goods, rock candy, and even his father's own brand of cough drops (note the "H.H. Cough Drops" on the last page) as well as "unique and fancy cabinets." Despite their continued best efforts, Hershey was out of business by May 1882.

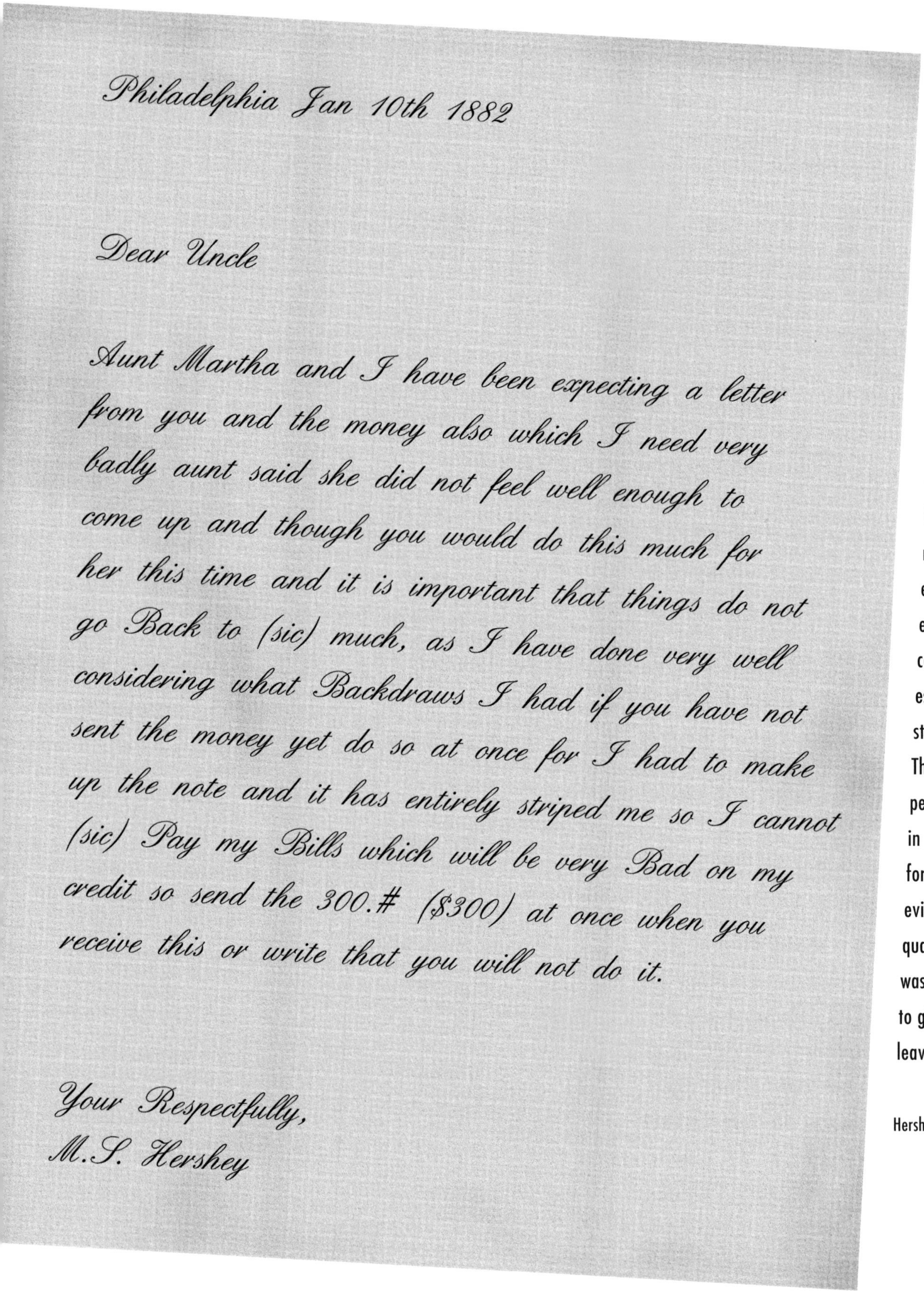

Philadelphia Jan 10th 1882

Dear Uncle

Aunt Martha and I have been expecting a letter from you and the money also which I need very badly aunt said she did not feel well enough to come up and though you would do this much for her this time and it is important that things do not go Back to (sic) much, as I have done very well considering what Backdraws I had if you have not sent the money yet do so at once for I had to make up the note and it has entirely striped me so I cannot (sic) Pay my Bills which will be very Bad on my credit so send the 300.# ($300) at once when you receive this or write that you will not do it.

Your Respectfully,
M.S. Hershey

Letter from Milton Hershey to his Uncle Abraham Snavely, dated January 10, 1882. Milton Hershey relied heavily upon the financial backing of his relatives to support his early business efforts. In each instance, Hershey constantly struggled to establish enough credit to stabilize his cash flow. This letter reveals his desperate financial situation in Philadelphia; his lack of formal education is quite evident in its content and quality. One month after it was written, he was forced to give up his business and leave Philadelphia.

Hershey Community Archives

M.S. Hershey

A young man about age 22. He claims to have a capital about $5,000. Confessed he is mostly furnished by an aunt, Mrs. Snavely who holds a judgment on him for $3000. Doing a fair business, but making no money. He is considered industrious, attentive, hardworking, and honest. Sells low, although obtaining some credit. Not considered desirable as judgment could be closed on him at any time.
January 18, 1880   Spring Garden St.

M.S. Hershey

He has been under large expenses here and giving up retail business. Intends going to wholesale business exclusively at Beach Street above Marlboro. His capital is secured by a relative. Is considered honest and so far has paid for what he has bought. So far he has made 0 in this retail business, but it is made left to see how he will do in his new enterprise. We can only suggest care in transactions at the present time.
May 5, 1881

M.S. Hershey
Confessed judgment of $3000 to M.B. Snavely.
January 19, 1882

Dunn & Bradstreet Credit Ledgers, Vol. 17, page 391, Philadelphia Index. Credit reports written by agents of Dunn & Bradstreet in the early 1880s show that Milton Hershey's increasingly precarious financial position was not unknown to the various banks and creditors in Philadelphia.

Hagley Museum and Library
Dunn & Bradstreet Credit Ledgers
Microfilm role 150, page 391

M.S. Hershey
Out of business.
May 23, 1882

Good material went into the caramel products of the Lancaster Caramel Company. There were, of course, different grades at different prices for different markets. One of the least expensive products was the *Unique*, which sold to children at eight for a penny. Medium-grade product included *Jim Crack* and *Roly Poly*. Other lines, such as *Empire* and *Melba*, were made with skim milk. The top of the *Crystal A* product line included *Cocoanut Ices*, *Paradox*, and *Lotus*. *Lotus* was made of sugar, corn syrup, whole milk, almonds, cocoa powder, and chocolate. The three-inch square *Lotus* caramel sold for one dollar for a five-pound box.

A NEW LIFESTYLE

Four years after returning penniless to Lancaster, Milton Hershey had become one of the city's most successful businessmen and prominent citizens. His company had quickly expanded to include plants in other Pennsylvania cities, as well as a western plant in Chicago, Illinois. Milton Hershey had become a millionaire with his integrity, sincerity, and simplicity of character fully intact. The financial success of the Lancaster Caramel Company gave Milton Hershey the freedom to explore other interests. He traveled extensively in this country and abroad. He took time off each year to travel to Europe, especially to England. Guided by his natural curiosity, Hershey visited museums, churches, and historic places, as well as other traditional tourist sites. His interest in the confectionery business may also have led him to visit European candy manufacturers. Mr. Hershey was a keen observer and little escaped his eye.

In 1891, Milton Hershey purchased a large mansion at 222 South Queen Street in Lancaster. He and his mother resided there. The house was located only a few blocks from the Caramel Company. Milton Hershey spent a great deal of time, effort, and money in selecting interior and exterior furnishings and decorations. He became interested in horses, riding, and carriages. He engaged an English coachman, joined the Lancaster Coaching Club, and participated in other upper-class amusements. With success, however, came change. In April 1894, Martha Snavely, one of his staunchest supporters and earliest benefactors, passed away. Then, on May 25, 1898, at the age 41, he surprised his family and friends by marrying Catherine "Kitty" Sweeney of Jamestown, New York, in the rectory of St. Patrick's Cathedral in New York. Although the exact circumstances of the courtship remain one of the holes in the Hershey story, his love for her and her memory is well documented.

Kitty Hershey was a beautiful, articulate, refined, and stylish Roman Catholic woman, as well as an accomplished amateur musician. It was not long before the personalities of Mother Hershey and Kitty Hershey clashed. Milton Hershey soon purchased his mother another home in Lancaster where she could live and tolerate her son's new wife at a close distance. Milton Hershey then turned his attention to bringing his father back to Pennsylvania and making the latter years of his life comfortable. He realized his parents would never again live under the same roof, and so he hit upon the idea of establishing his father in the old family Homestead in Derry Township. In April 1897, Milton Hershey repurchased the property and in 1898 his father returned from Colorado to live there until his death in 1904. By the end of 1898, Milton Hershey was certainly one of Lancaster's most substantial, successful, and happiest citizens. And even greater things were on the horizon.

Business Cards circa 1880.
With the help of his family, Milton Hershey managed to do a fair business, but made little money. He and his family worked long hours and by 1879 managed to secure more ambitious premises at 925–927 Spring Garden Street. Because of his low volume of business and limited cash flow, he often fell behind in his payments and lived in constant fear that impatient sugar dealers would suspend his supply of raw materials. In an effort to increase business, he set up a wholesale office at 532 Linden Street.

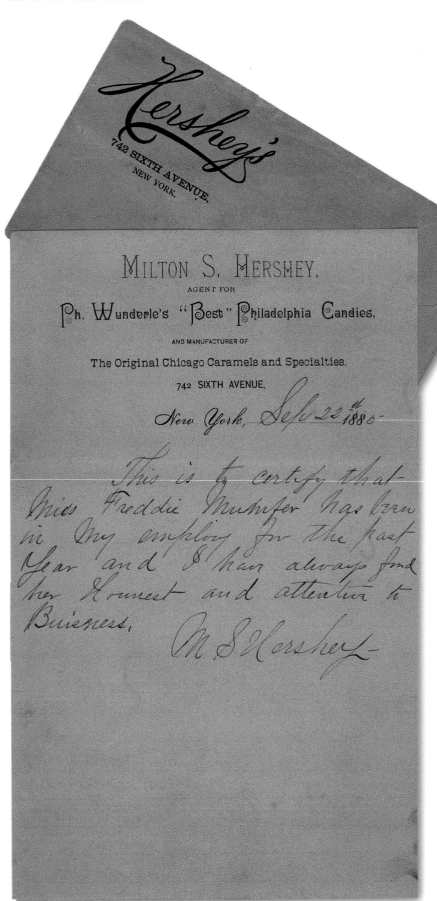

MILTON S. HERSHEY,

AGENT FOR

Ph. Wunderle's "Best" Philadelphia Candies,

AND MANUFACTURER OF

The Original Chicago Caramels and Specialties.

742 SIXTH AVENUE,

New York, Sep 22d 1885

This is to certify that Miss Freddie Mumfer has been in My employ for the past Year and I have always find her Honest and attentive to Buisness.

M S Hershey

This personal recommendation was written by Milton Hershey on letterhead from his New York business and dated September 22, 1885, less than a year before his return to Lancaster. Milton Hershey entered New York in 1883 as penniless as he had exited Philadelphia. Despite the continued support of his parents and Aunt Mattie, Hershey was once again hampered by the problems of small volume and little cash flow. After three years, he was forced to suspend his business operations and return to Lancaster with his family.

Caramels Only.

Consisting of THIRTY VARIETIES.

THE ONLY ORIGINAL UNWRAPPED CARAMELS

PACKED 196 IN A BOX,

ARE MANUFACTURED BY THE

Lancaster Caramel Company,

LANCASTER, PA.

N. Y. Office, 383 Canal Street.

And bear the Trade Mark,

CRYSTAL. A CONFECTIONS

All others are imitations.

Insist on having this brand if you wish to increase your trade on Caramels.

Please mention the CONFECTIONERS' JOURNAL when writing Advertisers.

Lancaster Caramel Company circa 1895. The company began in a small room at 355 Church Street and eventually extended 301 feet along Church Street to include 450,000 square feet of floor space.

Display Box circa 1890. Milton Hershey achieved his first success manufacturing and selling caramels under the *Crystal A* name. Retailers displayed product on retail shelves for purchase. Access was through a hinged glass door on the rear.

This ad is taken from the *Confectioners' Journal,* a trade publication. It is an early example of Milton Hershey's effort to capture a national market.

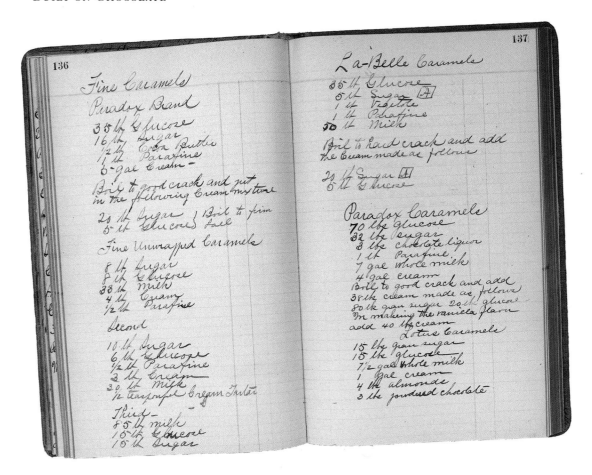

Formula Book 1897. This book was used to record product sales and recipes in the western (Chicago) plant of the Lancaster Caramel Company. The plant was managed by Frank Snavely, a cousin of Milton Hershey's, and may be in his own hand. The pages near the back of the book record the bulk caramel recipes for the product listed in the front sales portion. All of the recipes employ copious amounts of milk, whole milk, or cream—helping to ensure their freshness and delectability.

Milton Hershey's Lancaster Home. In 1891, Hershey purchased this home at 222 South Queen Street in Lancaster. He took great interest and pride in remodeling and furnishing the home. He filled it with exotic birds, plants, and mementos of his travels.

For most of the 1890s, Milton Hershey lived the carefree life of a Victorian bachelor. With one eye always paying careful attention to his business affairs, Hershey allowed himself the opportunity to enjoy some of the finer things in life that were now made available to him. He enjoyed filling his new home with expensive objects. For example, on August 25, 1892, he purchased a 24-tune, three-cylinder Swiss music box and accompanying inlay table from Henry Goutschi and Sons of Sainte Croixe, Switzerland, through their Philadelphia office for $708.25. The music box was the best money could buy, equipped with decorative bells, a snare drum attachment, and separate drawers for the storage of each music cylinder. He also joined private social and business clubs, including the Lancaster Coaching Club, and enjoyed taking trips to Europe and larger American cities, including Chicago in 1893 for the Colombian Exposition.

Milton Hershey loved to travel abroad. This passport, although from a later period of his life, is indicative of his favorite travel destinations. It shows that he traveled to France, the United Kingdom, Germany, and Spain in 1926.

Mr. Hershey purchased this minute-repeater pocket watch in Berlin, Germany, in 1892. Perhaps no other single object is more indicative of the new lifestyle afforded him by the success of the Lancaster Caramel Company. An exquisite and ostentatious timekeeping mechanism, it is activated by a small lever on the side which in turn activates three different bell tones marking the hour, quarter hour, and minute. By counting the tones, the owner can tell the time of day without opening the case. The intricate internal mechanisms also keep track of the days and months, and contain a stopwatch function as well. From Milton Hershey, the watch passed to his cousin Ezra F. Hershey, who was an officer of the Chocolate Company and the son of Elias Hershey. It has passed down through that branch of the Hershey family and has been on loan to the Hershey Museum from the family of Mrs. Betty Hershey Lutz for many years.

Made by Wedgwood, this 1894 plate was specifically designed and hand-painted for a dinner given in honor of Milton Hershey and hosted by the Lancaster Coaching Club. The names of each club member and the dinner menu are recorded on the front. South Central Pennsylvania towns visited by the club in their carriages are recorded on the reverse.

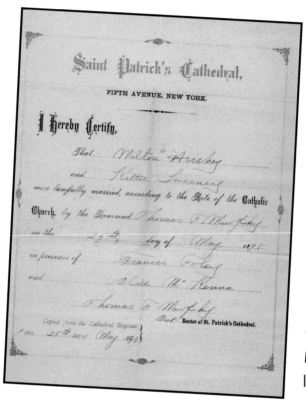

Milton S. Hershey and Catherine Sweeney were married in the rectory of St. Patrick's Cathedral in New York City on May 25, 1898. Since Milton Hershey was not a member of the Roman Catholic Church, the marriage was performed in the rectory. Mrs. Hershey remained a practicing Roman Catholic throughout most of her life. However, as her health deteriorated in the years immediately before her death, she turned to Christian Science.

Milton Hershey's philanthropy began soon after his marriage to Catherine. Perhaps the earliest recorded example of that generosity is Milton Hershey's substantial gift to Franklin and Marshall College in Lancaster circa 1900 for the construction of a laboratory (known as the Milton S. Hershey Chemical Laboratories) in the college's new Science Building. The June 1902 minutes of the board of trustees record that "the Chemical Department has been splendidly equipped by Milton S. Hershey of this city, the outfit costing about $5,000." According to a college publication of 1906, the Science Building was erected in 1900–01 at a total cost, with equipment, of about $75,000.

Coming only two years after their marriage in 1898, it would seem that Catherine played some part in this and later philanthropic undertakings of her husband. He himself said many times that the idea to create the Hershey Industrial School for orphaned boys (now the Milton Hershey School for underprivileged youth) was "Kitty's idea" and it is her name that appears as a contributor inside the main entrance to St. Patrick's Cathedral in Harrisburg, Pennsylvania. The extent of her influence will never be known, however, and is one of the holes in the Hershey story that may never be completely filled.

Young Milton Hershey circa 1863. This boyhood photograph was taken about the time that Milton Hershey began school. His formal education was constantly interrupted by frequent moves.

Milton Hershey, age 15 circa 1872.
The photograph was taken in the early 1870s when a teenaged Milton Hershey was apprentice to Joseph Royer in Lancaster, Pennsylvania.

Milton Hershey circa 1887. The Portrait and Biographical Record of Lancaster County, 1894 refers to Hershey as a successful businessman on his way to becoming "one of Lancaster's Most Substantial Citizens."

(Oval) *Milton Hershey circa 1905.*

Catherine Sweeney Hershey. The beautiful, vivacious "Kitty" Hershey was a striking contrast to Milton Hershey's mother in her plain dress and strict habits. The two women did not always get along. Milton Hershey met Kitty during his business trips, although exact circumstances of their courtship are not recorded. His marriage to the Roman Catholic Sweeney came as a great surprise to his fellow workers and especially to his mother.

Catherine Sweeney Hershey circa 1898. Milton Hershey's new bride.

(Above) The Hersheys in Nice, France, 1910; and (below) in Egypt, 1913. Mrs. Hershey loved to travel as much as her husband.

(Oval) A studio portrait taken on holiday.

Out and About circa 1910. Milton and Catherine Hershey both enjoyed traveling in automobiles. Even after Catherine's death, Milton Hershey continued to own a number of opulent vehicles and employed a chauffeur.

MILTON SNAVELY HERSHEY
Paternal Lineage

CHRISTIAN HERSHEY   Married

Born Switzerland   Details unknown

Birth date unknown

Died Chester County, Pennsylvania

1722

BENJAMIN HERSHEY   Married   **(1) MARY**

Born Switzerland   **(2) MAGDALENA RHOADE**

1696

Died Lancaster County, Pennsylvania

July 29, 1789

CHRISTIAN HERSHEY	Married	**(1) BARBARA HOSTETTER**
Born Lancaster County, Pennsylvania		**(2) ANNA HERNLEY**
February 21, 1719		1738–1812
Died Lancaster County, Pennsylvania		
November 21, 1782		

ISAAC HERSHEY	Married	**ANNA FRANTZ**
Born Lancaster County, Pennsylvania		Born Lancaster County, Pennsylvania
February 6, 1773		September 22, 1774
Died Dauphin County, Pennsylvania		Died Dauphin County, Pennsylvania
January 17, 1831		August 9, 1861

JACOB HERSHEY	Married	**NANCY HERSHEY**
Born Dauphin County, Pennsylvania	January 29, 1828	Born Lancaster County, Pennsylvania
September 22, 1802		January 22, 1808
Died Lebanon County, Pennsylvania		Died Dauphin County, Pennsylvania
May 15, 1877		September 3, 1869

HENRY HERSHEY	Married	**VERONICA (FANNY) SNAVELY**
Born Dauphin County, Pennsylvania	January 15, 1856	Born Lancaster County, Pennsylvania
January 4, 1829		September 14, 1835
Died Dauphin County, Pennsylvania		Died Dauphin County, Pennsylvania
February 18, 1904		March 11, 1920

MILTON S. HERSHEY	Married	**CATHERINE (KITTY) SWEENEY**
Born Dauphin County, Pennsylvania	May 25, 1898	Born Jamestown, New York
September 13, 1857		July 6, 1872
Died Dauphin County, Pennsylvania		Died Philadelphia, Pennsylvania
October 13, 1945		March 25, 1915

Chapter 2

Milk Chocolate
"A Sweet to Eat, A Food to Drink"

Torchère, Hershey Chocolate Company Soda Fountain and Candy Store 1901–1904. Milton Hershey purchased this cut glass torchère at the Chicago Colombian Exposition in 1893. Displayed by L. Strauss and Sons, New York, it is believed that the glass was manufactured in France by the Baccarat Company and shipped as pressed glass blanks to New York where Strauss carried out the intricate and detailed cutting of each piece. From 1901 until 1904, the torchère was displayed at the Hershey Chocolate Company showroom at 1020 Chestnut Street in Philadelphia. In 1909, it was installed in the foyer of High Point, the Hersheys' new home. It is a one-of-a-kind piece, indicative of the flamboyant lifestyle led by Milton Hershey in the 1890s, and contains 1,200 parts and weighs over 600 pounds.

"I AM GOING TO MAKE CHOCOLATE"

Admission Tickets, Colombian Exposition 1893. The 1893 Colombian Exposition was a celebration of international skill and enterprise. Visiting the Exposition, Milton Hershey was intrigued by a display of German chocolate-making equipment, which he bought and shipped to his Lancaster caramel factory. Once home, he began to experiment...

The rapid development of the chocolate-making industry in the late 19th century did not escape the keen confectioner's eye of Milton Hershey. The chocolate industry was booming and clearly chocolate was a confection of the future. American chocolate makers were hard-pressed to keep pace with a growing demand for cocoa, baking chocolate, and sweetened chocolate products. Hershey himself had seen the growing demand for chocolate coatings on his caramels. However, milk chocolate remained a handmade luxury item produced only in Europe with closely guarded secret formulas based on discoveries made by Daniel Peters, a Swiss, in 1876.

Milton Hershey was first exposed to the practical applications of chocolate making in 1893 when he visited the Colombian Exposition in Chicago with his cousin Frank Snavely, manager of the western branch of the Lancaster Caramel Company. Among its many and varied displays were machines celebrating international skill and enterprise. The exhibit that most attracted the attention of Milton Hershey was that on chocolate manufacturing shown by the J.M. Lehmann Company of Dresden, Germany. Impressed and intrigued by the display and its equipment, he purchased the necessary machinery, had it shipped to Lancaster, and began to experiment with making chocolate in the eastern end of his caramel manufactory. However, Milton Hershey was interested in producing more than the sweet chocolate novelties of his time. Hershey was confident he could eventually duplicate his success with fresh milk caramels and produce a quality mass-produced milk chocolate product that was also affordable.

In 1894, the Hershey Chocolate Company began producing sweet chocolate and cocoa for flavoring and coating Hershey's own caramels. When the caramel company began to produce more chocolate than it could use, Hershey hired William Murrie in early 1895 to sell the excess product to other confectioners. Murrie had been a successful salesman for Weaver and Costello, a rival candy manufacturer in Pittsburgh, Pennsylvania.

Murrie made the first recorded sale of *Hershey's* chocolate to an outside vendor on April 17, 1895. He quickly proved his worth to Milton Hershey and his company, and became a close business associate of Milton Hershey's, serving as president of the chocolate operation from 1908 until 1947. With the help of Murrie and others, the product line had quickly expanded to include breakfast cocoa and baking chocolate, as well as a variety of sweet chocolate novelties. During the first few years of its existence, the company made no attempt to market milk chocolate. The "Wholesale Price-List of *Hershey's* Fine Vanilla Chocolate Novelties and Fancy Packages" shows that Hershey produced 114 items in the Lancaster plant, offered in such a variety of colors, sizes, and wrappings as to double and then redouble the original figure. Many of the fanciful names and wrappers emulated the finest European boutique-style chocolates of the day and included Chocolate Cigars (with names like *Esquisitos, Cuban,* and *Hero of Manila*), Chocolate Cigarettes (with names like *Le Chat Noir, Opera, Smart Set,* and *Tennis*), *Bijous, Chocolate Blossoms, Sweet Peas,*

Souvenir Plate, Colombian Exposition 1893. This is an exterior view of Machinery Hall, which housed the chocolate-making display viewed by Milton Hershey.

Interior View of the 1893 Colombian Exposition's Machinery Hall, Extending Over 1,000 Feet in Length. "In this great building was a marvelous exhibit of the most perfect machinery ever devised by the genius of man, performing work with what seemed to be the highest intelligence, and exciting the amazement of visitors whichever way they turned to make their examinations."

Hershey Chocolate Company, Lancaster, Pennsylvania, 1895–1898. By 1895, the Hershey Chocolate Company was in full operation, supplying coatings for the Lancaster Caramel Company as well as selling chocolate to the outside market. Like other chocolate makers of the period, Hershey manufactured cocoa, baking chocolate, and a wide variety of sweet chocolate novelties. Not until 1900 did the company commercially manufacture milk chocolate.

Chrysanthemum, Chocolate Bicycles, Lady Fingers, College Wafers, Dominoes, Croquettes, Princess Wafers, and *Le Roi de Chocolate.*

By the late 1890s, this famous name in candy history—*Hershey's* milk chocolate—had yet to appear. Developing a formula and process to manufacture inexpensive milk chocolate presented exciting new challenges, but proved to be a complicated task. Today, it is hard to imagine how something as familiar as *Hershey's* milk chocolate could require so much time to develop. However, it was those very experiments that eventually established *Hershey's* milk chocolate as "First in Favor and Flavor." In 1899, after perfecting his own unique formula, Hershey began to produce milk chocolate. In February 1900, the Hershey Chocolate Company first marketed milk chocolate bars. *Hershey's* milk chocolate, then as now, appealed to consumers not only because it was delicious, fresh, and wholesome, but also because it provided the average person with a quality product and an opportunity to enjoy what up until then had been a luxury item.

ADVERTISING

In Lancaster, Hershey often advertised by conventional means in national trade publications such as the *Confectioners' Journal* to promote his chocolate products. Seeing the immediate popularity of milk chocolate, Hershey also aggressively pursued innovative and often expensive promotions to create and sustain an even greater demand. He realized that mass-producing a limited number of milk chocolate products in quantity would be more profitable than offering a greater variety of the less popular sweet chocolate novelties. By offering a smaller number of products, but producing them in larger volume, he realized he would lower his production costs per unit, which in turn would allow him to lower the cost of the product to the consumer. The lower cost would then fuel an even greater demand for the product. As early as February 1900, Milton Hershey began his effort to promote milk chocolate sales by bringing to Lancaster what is

reputed to be the first electric automobile ever used for business purposes. He used the automobile, a Riker Electric, to both advertise his business and to deliver his product. As part of a national marketing effort, Hershey wrapped in each bar of milk chocolate 1 from a series of 20 fanciful collector "bar cards" that touted the entire product line of the company. Targeting the largest consumer market, a Hershey Chocolate Company ledger entry for February 28, 1901, shows an entry for "New York Advertising" and the amount of $5,918.82. Hershey even had a sign erected on 110th Street in Manhattan advertising his new milk chocolate. An early advertising slogan describing *Hershey's* chocolate as "a palatable confection and a most nourishing food" became a description quickly condensed to the catchy "A Sweet to Eat, A Food to Drink."

THE DECISION

The immediate success of the Hershey Chocolate Company proved two things to Milton Hershey: first, that there was a market for affordable high-quality milk chocolate, and, second, that in order to take advantage of the demand for this product, he would need a much larger

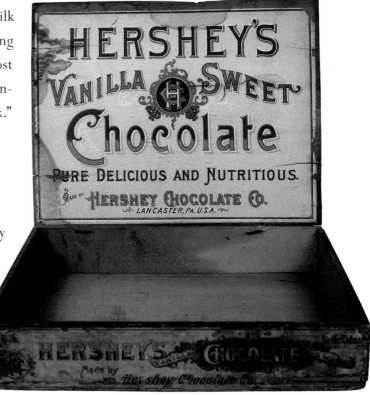

Machine-Dovetailed Wooden Display Box, Hershey Chocolate Company, Lancaster, Pennsylvania, 1895–1898. Manufacturers of all kinds used this type of hinged-lid display box to ship and display their products. By simply raising its lid, the shipping box made a handy self-contained point-of-purchase display for the retailer and a convenient advertising panel for the product's manufacturer.

Retail Display Box 1895–1898. Manufacturers have always used product packaging to help increase sales. Colorful illustrations and snappy slogans often accompanied claims of purity and quality. Because of Hershey's years of experience and quality ingredients, he could confidently assert his products to be of "Superior Quality and Excellency of Flavor" and "Warranted Absolutely Pure."

Retail Display Box, Magnolia Sweet Chocolate Fingers 1895–1898.

factory. By chance, in 1899, a group of rival caramel manufacturers headed by Dan Lafean of the American Caramel Company approached Milton Hershey with plans for a giant merger to control over 95 percent of the caramel-manufacturing industry. Hershey, though, was not interested in a merger. Instead, based on the success of his chocolate operation, he offered to sell his company to the American Caramel Company and in turn concentrate exclusively on the manufacture of chocolate. The negotiations were complicated and took over a year to complete.

But then, on August 10, 1900, Hershey announced the sale of the Lancaster Caramel Company to his major competitor for $1,000,000.

With the sale of the Lancaster Caramel Company, Hershey now had the money to expand his chocolate business. As part of the sales agreement for the building, machinery, warehouse stock, formulas, and trademarks of the caramel company, Hershey retained the right to continue manufacturing chocolate under the *Hershey's* name and to lease space in the caramel company building for his chocolate-making equipment until he could relocate to a larger building. While continuing to produce chocolate novelties and milk chocolate products in

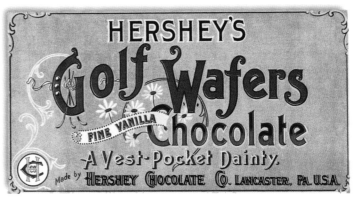

Lancaster, Milton Hershey carefully considered his options. After exploring several sites in and around Lancaster, Hershey decided to construct his new factory in a new location.

THE SEARCH

After considering several urban sites along the eastern seaboard, Milton Hershey rejected traditional urban locations for his chocolate factory and instead decided to place his business in the country. He chose a site in Derry Township near the Homestead, his childhood home, and the small village of Derry

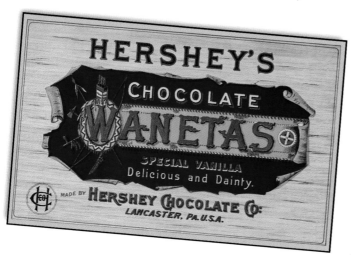

Church. Many of his friends and business associates thought he was foolish, but Milton Hershey had his reasons. He was, of course, familiar with the township from his childhood. He already owned some property in the

form of the Homestead, and the wide-open spaces offered the opportunity to purchase additional land at reasonable prices. Located in the heart of Pennsylvania German dairy country, Derry Township offered a plentiful supply of fresh milk unencumbered by competing industrial interests. In an area flanked by Harrisburg (the state capital) 12 miles to the west, and the cities of Lebanon 12 miles to the east and Lancaster 20 miles to the south, Derry Township also provided potential access to a steady and dependable labor force and access to urban regional rail transportation centers.

Golf Wafers 1895–1898.
Golf Wafers were one of many products the Hershey Chocolate Company marketed before the introduction of *Hershey's* milk chocolate bar in 1900. Golf was a popular sport of the rich and well-to-do at the turn of the century and the *Golf Wafers "Vest-Pocket Dainty"* heralded images of a country-club lifestyle and leisurely recreation.

Wanetas 1895–1898. Packaging such as that for *Wanetas* was designed to appeal to consumers' imaginations and conjured up images of adventure and the mysterious.

Little Puck Cigars 1895–1898.

Chocolate Segars 1895–1898. Chocolate cigars or "segars" and cigarettes were a popular part of the Hershey Chocolate Company's extensive product line. All of the chocolate products produced during this period were sweet chocolate, often flavored with vanilla. Hershey would not introduce milk chocolate until 1900.

PLANNING FOR A MODEL COMMUNITY

Hero of Manila Chocolate Segars circa 1898. This package of 12 chocolate cigars sought to capitalize on America's recent victory over Spain in the short Spanish-American War of 1898. Popular hero Admiral Dewey and his famous "Gridley, you may shoot when you are ready" declaration (uttered during the heat of battle in Manila Bay, the Philippines) grace the upper right corner of the label.

From the beginning, Milton Hershey planned to construct more than a large modern factory in Derry Township. The rural nature of the area meant that trolley and rail lines would need to be constructed to move laborers, raw materials, and product to and from the surrounding cities. Individuals and businesses would quickly flock to the area. A town with buildings, roads, and public works would naturally grow up around the factory. Why not create a model community—a City Beautiful? It was an ambitious undertaking and Milton Hershey was well aware of the potential risks and rewards.

On February 19, 1903, less than two months before breaking ground for construction of the new factory, an article appeared in the *Harrisburg Independent* entitled "A New Town Near Derry Church to Cost 1 Million: To Be Built by M.S. Hershey, The Chocolate Man" with the following information:

A new town which will have a population of 1500 will be built midway between Derry Church and Swatara, this county, along the line of the Philadelphia and Reading railway, by M.S. Hershey, the Lancaster chocolate manufacturer, who has large manufacturing interests in various parts of the state.

He has already begun work there on the erection of a new factory, which will employ 600 men, to supersede the plant at Lancaster, and his purpose in building the new town is to form a modern dwelling community for his employees and their families. Mr. Hershey has planned an expenditure of $1,000,000 to further his enterprise....

The town will be laid out along plans of modern manufacturing communities which are now springing up, all over this country, patterned after those in England. It will contain grass plots for pleasure parks in which there will be fountains and stone walks. The streets will be made of crushed stone taken from the quarries and stone crushing machinery has already been installed....

Milton Hershey's interest in the welfare of his workers and in creating an aesthetically pleasing "model town" was neither unique or unprecedented. However, the town of Hershey became unique because it reflected the unique beliefs and personality of its creator. Milton Hershey took a personal interest in his town and its inhabitants. He encouraged individuals to own their own homes. He created the Hershey Improvement Company to build roads and buildings. Under the umbrella of the Hershey Chocolate Company, Mr. Hershey provided all the support services needed to run a

Le Roi de Chocolate Tablets 1895–1898. During the 19th century, chocolate was considered to be a luxury item. When Milton Hershey began making chocolate in 1894, he chose names for his products that suggested a wealthy or select image. Products were sometimes named for colleges (*Vassar Gems*), leisure activities (*Golf Wafers, Tennis Cigarettes*), or European royalty (*La Grand Duchess, Le Roi de Chocolate*).

Vassar Gems 1895–1898. Among the more popular "collegiate" chocolates, *Vassar Gems* were developed with women in mind and named for the well-known all-girls' school. The product was packaged in boxes decorated with flowers and feminine colors.

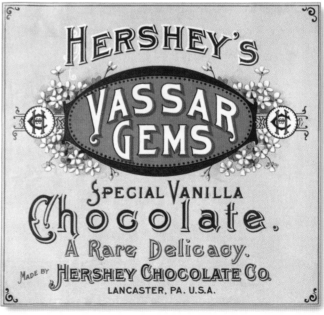

town. The Chocolate Company managed the utilities and various recreational facilities, including a zoo, park, and inn, while providing for trolley, laundry, and banking services. Milton Hershey also supported town-sponsored organizations such as the volunteer fire department, the public library, and men's and women's clubs, often providing them with buildings and offering financial support as well.

In realizing his dream, Milton Hershey became an innovative urban planner as well as a successful confectioner and entrepreneur. Under his guidance, the town of Hershey quickly became "Chocolatetown, U.S.A.!" and its tree-lined park "The Sweetest Park on Earth." *Hershey's* milk chocolate and the legacy it created were here to stay.

Chocolate Croquettes 1895–1898. During its first years, the Hershey Chocolate Company produced over 200 items varying in formula, shape, and packaging. Croquettes were a very popular confectionery shape. Hershey manufactured chocolate croquettes until the 1920s, long after other novelty shapes had been discontinued.

Chocolate Fans 1895–1909. This box contained nine wedge-shaped chocolate pieces around a small semicircular center to form a handheld fanlike pattern. Each piece was highly decorated with detailed fanciful designs, produced in a European-made mold.

DATING THE HERSHEY CHOCOLATE COMPANY'S LANCASTER ADVERTISING AND PRODUCT PACKAGING

Even after the 1905 opening of the new factory in Hershey, Pennsylvania, Milton Hershey continued to manufacture chocolate novelty products and fancy goods in Lancaster until 1909, albeit on a much-diminished scale. From 1895 through 1898, products made in Lancaster utilized the stylized "H. C. Co." logo of the Hershey Chocolate Company. On August 1, 1898, Hershey adopted the "Baby-in-the-Bean" or "Child-in-the-Cocoa-Bean-Pod" trademark, which was

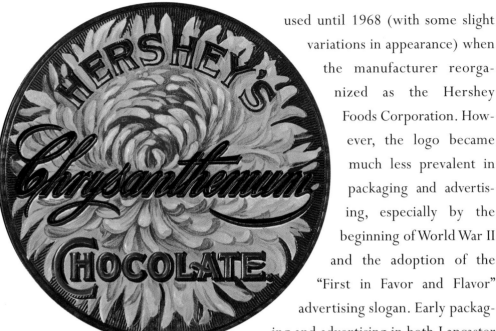

used until 1968 (with some slight variations in appearance) when the manufacturer reorganized as the Hershey Foods Corporation. However, the logo became much less prevalent in packaging and advertising, especially by the beginning of World War II and the adoption of the "First in Favor and Flavor" advertising slogan. Early packaging and advertising in both Lancaster and Hershey often show a single letter "A" surrounded by what appears to be a stylized series of concentric circles. Closer examination will show that the image actually spells out the word COCOA, a reference to the most essential ingredient and important product of the chocolate-manufacturing process.

Chrysanthemum Chocolate 1896–1909. In Lancaster, the Hershey Chocolate Company produced over 200 novelty chocolate products in a variety of formulas, shapes, and packages. This particular package contained eight pie-shaped sections around a circular center, all decorated to look like the leaves of a chrysanthemum.

Smart Set Cigarettes 1896–1905. The Hershey Chocolate Company manufactured many varieties of chocolate cigarettes and cigars. Chocolate cigarettes were largely marketed to women as an alternative to smoking tobacco products.

1895–1898	"H.C. Co." logo.
1898–1968	"Baby-in-the-Bean" trademark.

1895–1909   Baking chocolate, cocoa, and sweet chocolate novelties manufactured in Lancaster.

1900–1905   Milk chocolate bars and coatings manufactured in Lancaster. No record of milk chocolate bars being manufactured in Lancaster after the opening of the chocolate plant in Hershey in June 1905. However, price lists from the period mention milk chocolate coatings as a Hershey Lancaster product through 1909.

1905–Present   Milk chocolate bars and coatings manufactured in Hershey.

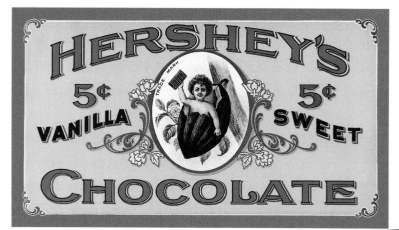

Vanilla Sweet Chocolate 1898–1905. This was the Hershey Chocolate Company's first confectionery product. The Chocolate Company was established in 1894 as an offshoot of Milton Hershey's highly successful Lancaster Caramel Company. The success of the Caramel Company supported Milton Hershey while he perfected his formula for milk chocolate.

National Chocolate Tablets 1895–1900.
At a time when people began to take physical fitness, athletics, and professional sports seriously, commercially processed foods were often touted as providing wholesome and nutritious quick energy for the sportsman or athlete.

Sweet Peas 1895–1909. Before Milton Hershey focused his energies on milk chocolate, the Hershey Chocolate Company's products followed the confectionery trends of the day: manufacturing and marketing a variety of chocolate novelties. Many of these products were marketed toward women and were produced in bite-sized pieces and packaged in more decorative boxes.

Milk Chocolate 1903–1905. The *Hershey's* milk chocolate bar we enjoy today was first introduced in 1900. Milton Hershey was the first American to develop a formula for milk chocolate. It took several years of experimentation before he perfected a formula that tasted good and remained fresh for a significant period of time.

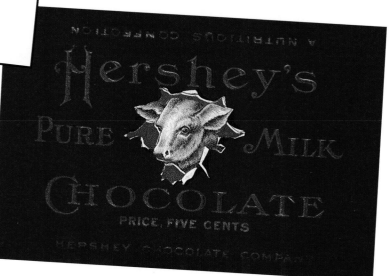

Cocoa 1898–1905. Hershey has continuously manufactured powdered cocoa since 1894. The company adopted the distinctive "Child-in-the-Cocoa-Bean-Pod" trademark in 1898 and it appeared on cans of *Hershey's* cocoa until 1936, when the company adopted the familiar block-style lettering still in use today.

Bittersweet Cocoa and Chocolate Advertisement 1896–1898. This design was first used on *Royal Cocoa* tins. It was also used as an advertising form. One product on the table is the vanilla sweet chocolate bar, the very first type of eating chocolate that Milton Hershey made in Lancaster, Pennsylvania. The reverse of the advertisement heralds the virtues of cocoa—specifically *Hershey's* cocoa. Chocolate quickly became "A Sweet to Eat" and cocoa "A Food to Drink" in early *Hershey's* product advertising.

Don't wreck your nerves with tea and coffee, or ruin your stomach with trashy substitutes. . . . . COCOA is a NATURAL FOOD DRINK, it makes RICH BLOOD and STRONG NERVES. . . **Hershey's Cocoa** is most efficient, because PURE.

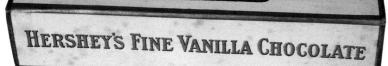

Product Packaging 1895–1909. The boutique-style specialty sweet chocolate novelties Milton Hershey produced in Lancaster were influenced by the European-style fancy boxed candies of the period. In order to increase production efficiency in his new factory in Hershey, Milton Hershey eliminated the fancy-shaped boxes and packaging in favor of high-quality, standard bar–shaped packaging.

Milk Chocolate Advertisement February 1905. A flyer announces a promotion for cakes of *Hershey's* milk chocolate in cooperation with a local Lancaster retailer.

Milk Chocolate Advertisement 1900–1905. Like many of his contemporaries, Hershey used advertising to promote the "nutritious" properties of both chocolate and cocoa. This early advertisement urges the consumer to try *Hershey's* milk chocolate for breakfast, lunch, and dinner. The "Baby-in-the-Bean" logo is clearly highlighted on the front, while the reverse features stylized concentric letter imagery to spell the word COCOA—two of the Hershey Chocolate Company's earliest and most prominent advertising images.

"Bar Card" Advertisement 1900–1905. To help promote sales of the new milk chocolate line in 1900, lithographed collector's cards were placed inside each piece of *Hershey's* milk chocolate.

BANANA

Riker Electric Automobile 1900. Milton Hershey is credited with bringing the first automobile to Lancaster. The Riker Electric Vehicle Company manufactured the automobile, which was used to advertise and deliver *Hershey's* products. Local newspapers noted the vehicle was equipped with lights, an electric bell, a brass "steering apparatus," and brakes. It could carry a load of approximately 2,000 pounds and had a storage battery with enough power to go 30 miles at a top speed of nine miles per hour. Milton Hershey paid nearly $2,000 for the vehicle and first put it into service on February 13, 1900.

"Three Friends" Advertisement circa 1900. "Three Friends" is a rare and early example of Hershey's turn-of-the-century promotional art. Nostalgic in tone, it was a point-of-sale poster, used in about 1900 when Hershey was still making cocoa and milk chocolate in Lancaster. Note the appearance of the stylized cocoa lettering on the young girl's sweater.

Tin Advertising Sign 1895–1898.

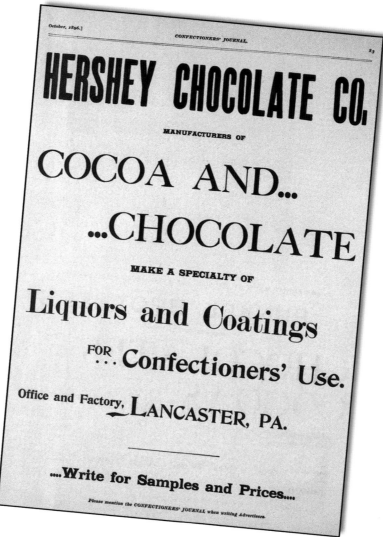

Wholesale Advertisement 1896. A national advertising piece for the Hershey Chocolate Company, Lancaster, Pennsylvania, which appeared in the trade publication *Confectioners' Journal* in October 1896 before the sale of the Lancaster Caramel Company and the introduction of milk chocolate bars. As an experienced confectioner, Milton Hershey realized the importance of establishing a viable wholesale trade. Hershey continued to sell chocolate coatings to outside candy makers well after Milton Hershey's own death in 1945.

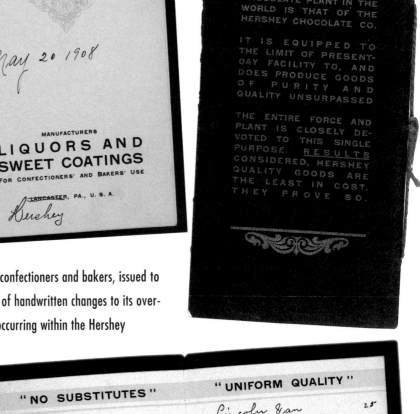

This 1908 House of Hershey wholesale price list for the use of confectioners and bakers, issued to a company salesman for use on his rounds, contains a number of handwritten changes to its overall text. These changes provide some insight into the changes occurring within the Hershey Chocolate Company between 1905 and 1908 as the company moved to the new factory in Hershey and began to phase out its Lancaster operations. The original text of the booklet is dated January 1905 and lists Lancaster, Pennsylvania, as the company's home. On the first page of the booklet, the date of May 20, 1908, has been added, and "Lancaster" has been crossed out and "Hershey" written beneath it in ink. Between 1905 and 1908, a number of products have been added or dropped and product costs have increased (and in some cases decreased), according to various handwritten additions. While the booklet makes no mention of milk chocolate bars, it does state that milk chocolate coatings were produced in Lancaster during these years, presumably until the operation ceased to exist in 1909.

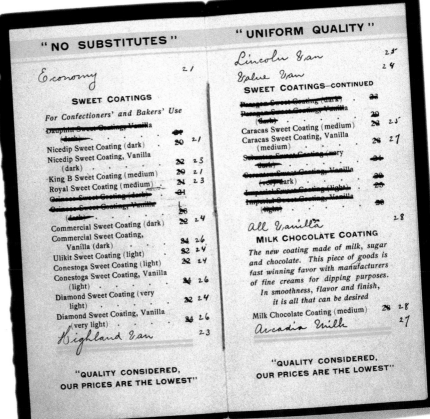

The "Baby-in-the-Bean" Logo. The Hershey Chocolate Company adopted the "Baby-in-the-Bean" company trademark on August 1, 1898. Until Hershey retired the image in 1968 when it reorganized as the Hershey Foods Corporation, the trademark underwent many subtle changes throughout the years. For example, the raised arm of the baby could hold a simple cup of cocoa, a steaming cup of cocoa, or an unwrapped chocolate bar. Sometimes even the physical appearance, facial expression, complexion, or hair of the child would change.

Birth and Baptismal Certificate, Derry Township 1741. The certificate below, or *taufscheine*, was printed as a blank by Barton and Jungmann of Reading, Pennsylvania, and completed by the artist Frederick Speyer for Johannes Bress of Derry Township. The Pennsylvania German residents of the area typically recorded important family events such as birth, baptism, marriage, and death on certificates like this.

Derry Church Advertisement circa 1895. (Above) Derry Church, the small community adjacent to the new factory, was settled by Scottish-Irish, German, and Swiss pioneers in the early 1700s. The community's economy was based on farming and stone quarrying. The quarries attracted significant numbers of Italian immigrants as laborers in the late 19th and early 20th centuries. Derry Church existed as a crossroads community until the establishment of the town of Hershey in 1903.

Chapter 3

From Beans to Bars
The Chocolate-Making Process

Packaging Cocoa circa 1920. The oldest product manufactured by Hershey Chocolate is *Hershey's* cocoa. To make it, cocoa beans must be roasted, shelled, ground, and pressed to remove the cocoa butter. The solid cakes left after the pressing are then ground into a fine powder and packaged in tins to keep the cocoa fresh.

The production of chocolate is more than a series of manufacturing steps. It takes people to make a quality product: to run the machines, correct the mistakes, and oversee quality. Like most businesses, Hershey Chocolate began as a small concern with a limited number of employees. With the phenomenal growth of the company, policies and practices soon needed to be quantified and codified. In 1947, the Hershey Chocolate Corporation issued its first employee handbook, "Working at Hershey." The handbook was a large folio, consisting

The Gift of Montezuma

Chocolate is produced by grinding roasted cocoa beans. A cocoa bean is composed of over 50 percent vegetable fat, called cocoa butter. As the bean is ground and heat is released, the cocoa butter melts. The result is a thick, bitter-tasting liquid that is normally mixed with other ingredients to produce a palatable food. The Aztecs were the first to discover the unique qualities of chocolate and cocoa butter. They discovered that cocoa butter does not dissolve when mixed with other ingredients, but remains in suspension in what chemists refer to as an emulsion. They also observed that cocoa butter has a relatively low melting point (about the same temperature as that of the human mouth) and so will return to a solid state at room temperature. The Aztecs combined crushed chocolate with water to concoct a frothy drink that was whipped with a special paddle to break up the suspended globules of cocoa butter. To cut the richness of the drink, the Aztecs

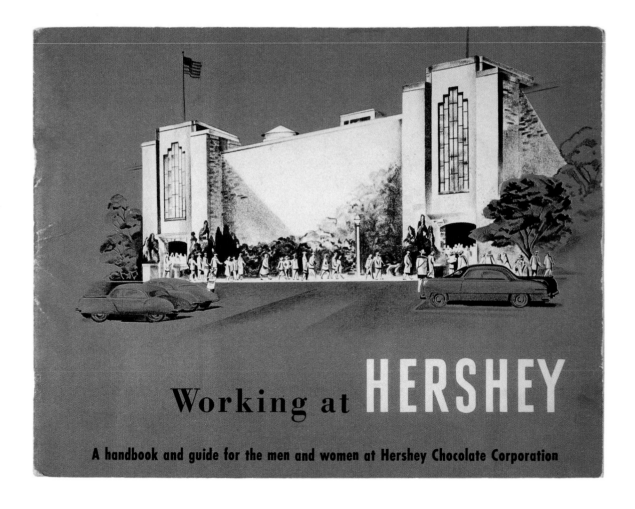

Working at **HERSHEY**

A handbook and guide for the men and women at Hershey Chocolate Corporation

often stirred in corn flour. Nevertheless, much of the cocoa butter would remain suspended, skimmed from the top, and discarded. According to legend, the paddle made a "choco-choco" sound and is the basis for the Spanish word *chocolatl* and the inspiration for the English word *chocolate*. Convinced of the divine qualities of chocolate, the Aztec emperor Montezuma reportedly consumed 50 goblets of the concoction every day.

When the Spanish brought chocolate to Europe in the early 16th century, it remained a popular drink rather than an edible food for over 300 years! Then, in 1828, C.J. Van Houten, a Dutch chemist, invented a hydraulic press that squeezed out about two-thirds of the cocoa butter from chocolate, leaving a chocolate powder we today call cocoa as well as solid cakes of cocoa butter. By a process known as "Dutching," in honor of Van Houten, he added dry alkaline substances to cocoa to make it better tasting and more soluble in water. Thanks to Van Houten's extracting press, other entrepreneurs soon discovered that adding additional quantities of cocoa butter to chocolate and refining it with sugar eliminated the bitter qualities of chocolate and resulted in the sweet chocolate or dark chocolate products manufactured by Hershey and other chocolate manufacturers in the late 19th century. In producing sweet chocolate products, manufacturers add small amounts of vanillin and other flavorings to add variety to their basic product. Taste and appearance is also affected by the content of added cocoa butter. Generally speaking, cocoa butter content increases as the product goes from extra-bittersweet to sweet and from dark to light.

The production of sweet chocolate and milk chocolate share many of the same manufacturing steps. While the technology used in making chocolate has undergone significant technological changes in the 100 years since Milton Hershey purchased his first equipment in 1893 at the Colombian Exposition, the basic processes have remained largely unchanged. Cocoa beans are still harvested largely by hand from trees in countries lying between 10 degrees north and 10 degrees south of the equator. Cocoa beans from different countries and latitudes contain different percentages of cocoa butter, which affect their taste and blending qualities. The blends of beans required by chocolate manufacturers, as well as the specifics of their individual processes, are closely guarded company secrets. However, some basic manufacturing steps are followed by all chocolate manufacturers.

of 32 pages, measuring 11 inches in height by 15 inches in width. The handbook contained separate sections on work and wages, job security, getting ahead, health and safety, holidays and vacations, attendance, leaves of absence, quality and production, the company–union relationship, social and recreational facilities, benefits for the serviceman, and complaints and grievances. In an effort to promote a sense of community, the handbook contained a chronological list of every employee currently working or retired from the plant beginning in 1905 and extending through 1947.

Once ripe pods are hand-harvested from cocoa trees, they are first split open to reveal 30–40 white cocoa beans. These beans are scooped from the pod, piled on the ground, covered with banana leaves, and left to ferment for several days until they become light brown in color. To further reduce their moisture content, beans are then spread out to dry in the tropical sun. Jute bags filled with dried beans are then shipped to processing plants like Hershey's, where they are cleaned and sorted by size. Next, they are roasted to bring out their full flavor and aroma. The intensity of the roast is different for each variety of bean and is also dependent on its expected use. After roasting, the shells of each bean are brittle and loose. A winnowing machine cracks open the beans and the loosened husk is blown away with a controlled air current. The remaining nibs are mixed and ground by still another machine, which generates enough heat in the process to melt the cocoa butter in each bean. The resulting liquid is a deep-colored paste called chocolate liquor (liquor in the old sense of the word, meaning liquid essence, not alcohol). If allowed to harden as it cools to room temperature, it forms baking chocolate, which is chocolate in its purest form; it is too dry and bitter to be eaten as is with any enjoyment.

Most chocolate liquor does not become powdered cocoa and cakes of cocoa butter, sweet chocolate, or baking chocolate. Instead, it becomes the basic ingredient for the best-selling chocolate of all time—milk chocolate—when combined with additional cocoa butter, sugar, and milk. The size of the sugar granule, as measured in microns, and the form of milk added to the chocolate liquor is different for each chocolate manufacturer and are key factors in determining the taste and texture of the final product. A few manufacturers, such as Hershey, use condensed liquid milk rather than the powdered dry milk preferred by the majority of manufacturers. As a rule, most European chocolates contain a smaller-sized granule of sugar to produce a smoother texture compared with that favored by American consumers. Whatever the form of the ingredients, they are kneaded together in giant mixers, refined, and "conched" to achieve the consummate silky texture of milk chocolate. Traditionally, conches are large rectangular troughs lined with granite over which granite rollers move back and forth over the chocolate mixture, though newer conches can be in the shape of round drums lined with state-of-the-art materials.

The introduction to "Working at Hershey" is provided by P.A. Staples, Chairman of the Board and President, Hershey Chocolate Corporation. His conservative corporate philosophy pays homage to the corporate legacy of Milton Hershey and his own efforts to maintain that success in the face of changing economic conditions in post–World War II America.

To everyone at Hershey Chocolate

From all over the world people come to visit Hershey.

They don't come just because we make chocolate bars or because Hershey is the leader of this important industry.

They come to see Hershey, one of the wonders of the industrial world. And they leave with the feeling that they have seen a remarkable sight, and how fortunate people are who work and live here. We all know how over a half century ago a man of vision and courage broke ground in this rich farming area to build more than just another business. He wanted to carry out an idea—to create a real opportunity for people to work successfully and to live well. There are nearly four thousand of us here today at the Hershey Chocolate Corporation to show that this idea really worked.

But our job at Hershey will never be fully done. In this modern world with its changing conditions, new problems and opportunities face us every day. To meet them and solve them is our big chance. Those of you with the Company for a long time can remember when operations were small. No written explanation was needed then to describe our privileges and tasks. But now that thousands of us are working here together, this manual has been prepared so that each will understand his rights and responsibilities, how his work and behavior affect others, how to avoid friction and misunderstanding and make it easier to progress together.

This manual is not a new set of rules and regulations. What it does is to set down those practices and policies which experience has already proved to be sound. When changes occur that affect us, when we learn better ways of doing things, the manual will be improved.

The purpose of this manual is to smooth the way, to help all of us do our part. Read it, consult it, discuss it with your associates. Every feature of it has a bearing on our joint success.

Yours Sincerely,

P.A. Staples
Chairman of the Board and President
Hershey Chocolate Corporation

Up to this point in the manufacturing process, the chocolate has been kept in its fluid state at temperatures up to 185°F. In the tempering process, the chocolate is cooled in a controlled manner that prevents the cocoa butter from recrystalizing later and making the finished chocolate grainy or discolored. The freshly tempered chocolate is just the right consistency to flow through molding machines to produce the various bars and other chocolate confections enjoyed by consumers all over the world.

THE FORMULA FOR SUCCESS

Employee Pay Tokens circa 1920s. Tokens were sometimes given to "piece" workers on the line who received them in proportion to the amount of processed product. Tokens were kept during the pay period and then redeemed for cash, trade, or merchandise. On the *Kisses* chocolates line, 20 dozen *Kisses* were equal to a 10-cent token. Denominations ranged from 1/4 cent to $300.00.

Milton Hershey's greatest contribution to the food industry was in the manufacture of milk chocolate. He was not, of course, the first to make it. Swiss confectioners Daniel Peters, Henri Nestle, and Rodolphe Lindt, among others, discovered the process for manufacturing milk chocolate with powdered milk. Milton Hershey, however, was the first to make it commercially, in mass, and out of fresh milk. No one taught him how to make milk chocolate with fresh milk or how to produce it in mass quantities. However,

Milk Delivery Trucks circa 1918. Fresh milk has always been a key ingredient in making *Hershey's* milk chocolate. Dairy farms surround the town of Hershey. In the early years of factory operations, milk was delivered by trucks and by trolley lines constructed by Milton Hershey to connect the community and factory with neighboring towns.

based on his own experience with caramels, he believed he could make milk chocolate with condensed fresh milk. He soon embarked on a series of experiments using condensing kettles to remove most of the moisture from milk. After finding a solution, he experimented with ways to successfully mix the condensed milk with chocolate liquor, sugar, and additional quantities of liquid cocoa butter to produce a quality milk chocolate.

Milton Hershey's first experiments in condensing fresh milk occurred in Lancaster. After he sold the caramel company, Milton Hershey built a small experimental condensing plant at the Homestead. At first, he tried to condense both cream and whole milk. Both processes were failures, turning milk chocolate rancid in a very short period. Finally, he discovered that skim milk worked best. To utilize the excess cream separated from the skim milk, Hershey set up a creamery and made butter. He then turned his attention to the problem of when to add the sugar to his mixture. Common sense seemed to dictate that it be added after the milk was condensed. However, Hershey found that he did not get enough moisture removed from the milk unless sugar was added to the milk before condensing. The process eventually perfected by Milton Hershey to manufacture his milk chocolate at the turn of the century is essentially the same process still used in the Hershey plants today. In the first step, known as "first mixing," chocolate

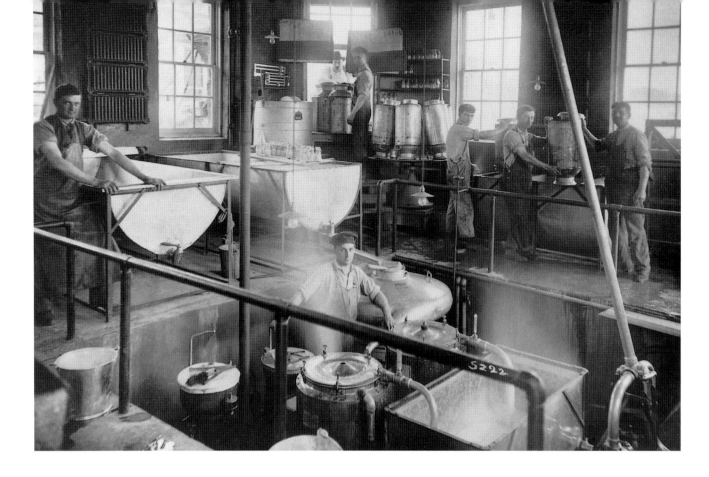

Milk Condensing Room circa 1910. With milk shipments arriving daily from surrounding farms, the factory milk room (where milk was condensed) ran on a very tight schedule. According to a company promotional text of 1926, every morning "60,000 gallons of fresh, creamy milk from grass-fed Holsteins were delivered to the factory, where they were pumped into condensers before combining with powdered sugar."

liquor is mixed with the condensed milk and sugar mixture in a "plow machine" until it becomes stiff. The mixture is then piped to "chasers" where it is ground into a fine powder called cocoa powder. In the second mixing, *mélangers* blend the chocolate powder with the proper amount of liquid cocoa butter. It is then piped to "roll refiners" where it is ground to a fine consistency between a series of steel rolls and mixed with vanilla flavoring. The resulting mixture is pumped into conches where it remains for several days to be further refined to a velvety smoothness. The product is then tempered, molded, wrapped, and shipped.

"THE GREAT AMERICAN CHOCOLATE BAR"

Molded chocolate in the form of the candy bar is the most straightforward product made from conched and tempered milk chocolate. The Hershey reputation rests squarely upon the most successfully mass-produced chocolate bar in the world: *Hershey's* milk chocolate. To create a *Hershey's* chocolate bar, a depositor, or pouring machine, is positioned above a continuously moving conveyor belt of bar-sized molds. A precisely timed jet of chocolate fills each mold before it is moved along the belt to a vibrating

The Round Barn circa 1925.

Cows Grazing on a Hershey Farm circa 1925.

machine that shakes the molds to spread the chocolate evenly and get rid of any air bubbles. Then the mold, still on the conveyor belt, travels to a cooling tunnel where the chocolate hardens. The solid bars are lifted out of their mold and sent off to packaging machines to be wrapped, boxed, shipped, and eagerly consumed the world over.

From its introduction to the present, *Hershey's* milk chocolate has been the choice of millions of consumers. "Give them quality," Milton Hershey once said. "That's the best kind of advertising in the world." Public acceptance of the "*Hershey's* taste" is without a doubt one of the greatest assets that Hershey Foods Corporation owns today. Thanks to the immediate acceptance of Mr. Hershey's first chocolate products—including *Hershey's* cocoa, baking chocolate, and milk chocolate—Milton Hershey set out to construct in the middle of a cornfield what would become the largest chocolate factory in the world.

"Chocolate and Cocoa—Nourishing Foods." The Educational and Dietetic Bureau of the Hershey Chocolate Corporation first published this linen-backed lithographed poster for use in public schools in the 1910s. Subsequent versions of the poster appeared throughout the 1950s and often included various elements reprinted from earlier versions. This 1955 version, for example, shows a map of pre–World War I Europe and a view of the factory and product packaging from the late 1930s. The poster includes information on the history and countries of origin of cocoa; a map of the world showing the names and origins of Hershey cocoa beans; an image of the factory in downtown Hershey; and a detailed eight-step breakdown of the process used by Hershey to turn raw cocoa beans into molded chocolate. The poster was intended to be used as a classroom teaching aid, alone or in conjunction with an educational booklet and exhibit entitled "The Story of Chocolate and Cocoa."

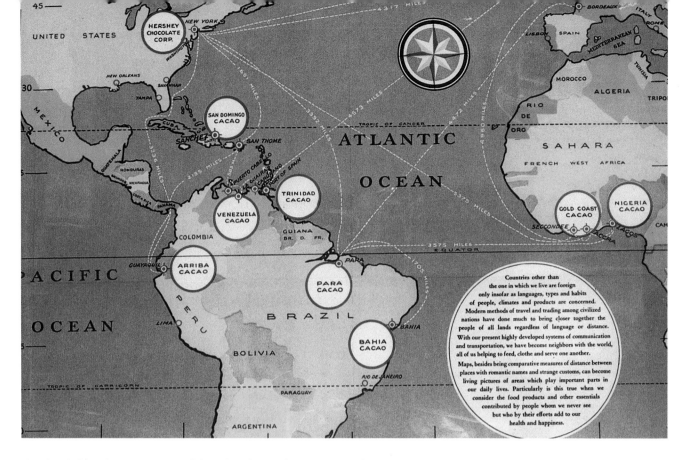

This detail, from the 1955 reprint of the "Chocolate and Cocoa—Nourishing Foods" poster, shows places in the world associated with the manufacture of *Hershey's* chocolate.

This detail, from the same poster, depicts the factory and product packaging circa the late 1930s.

Harvesting Cacao Pods. The cultivated cocoa tree grows to a height of 25 feet, has large leaves, and differs from our fruit trees in that the cacao pods, which are the fruit of the tree, grow on its trunk and main branches. At almost any time of the year, it is possible to see the small bright red blossoms, the growing pods, and the ripened fruit all present on the tree. The unripe pods are dark green but, as they mature, pass through successive stages of yellow, orange, red, and, finally, dark maroon. The yield of the trees averages 20 to 30 pods weighing a pound each. These are removed by means of a sharp knife attached to the end of a sharp pole called a *podadera*, inasmuch as the tree is not strong enough to bear climbing.

Removing Beans from the Pod. Cacao pods are from six to eight inches in length and from two to five inches in diameter. They are cut open with a small curved knife manipulated by a neat turn of the wrist. Within are found 20 to 40 white beans surrounded by a sticky pulp. In English-speaking countries, the bean is commonly called "cocoa." Upon removal from the pod, the beans are spread out to undergo a fermentation process, which changes the color from white to brownish red. After curing and drying, the beans are placed in large jute bags and are ready for shipment.

Roasting Cocoa Beans. When received in the modern chocolate factory, cocoa beans are first cleaned by going over a series of vibrating screens through which fall undersized beans and foreign substances, such as small twigs and stones. Strong air currents aid in the cleaning operations that precede the roasting process. The latter takes place in revolving drums through which air heated to a temperature of more than 300°F is drawn. This process facilitates later removal of the shells from the beans, removes moisture, and develops the color and flavor of the edible portions.

Milling or Grinding Cocoa Nibs. Removal of the shells results in the cracking of the kernels into small angular fragments called nibs. This material—the "meat" of the bean—is ground by being passed through milling machines that consist of three sets of steel-encased granite burr stones that revolve at a rapid rate. The friction heat generated by the grinding process causes the cocoa butter, making up more than half of the nibs, to melt, thus producing a smooth free-flowing chocolate liquor, the basis of all forms of chocolate.

Manufacturing Cocoa Powder. The most popular form of chocolate for beverage purposes is the familiar breakfast cocoa powder. Its preparation involves the reduction of the amount of fat present in the chocolate liquor and is accomplished in huge hydraulic presses. The chocolate liquor is conveyed to these heavy-duty machines and subjected to the enormous pressure of 6,000 pounds per square inch. Thus a portion of the cocoa butter, a pale yellow fluid when warm, is expressed, leaving behind the cocoa cakes that are then crushed, cooled, and sifted into a fine, soft, rich brown powder.

Processing Wholesome Milk. In the modern dairy, strictest attention is given to maintaining the high standards of cleanliness demanded in the production of fine quality milk chocolate. Whether or not milk is fit for human consumption depends entirely on thorough sanitation and a production process subject to the highest quality controls. Pure milk is an excellent source of protein, fat, and carbohydrate, the three main ingredients that supply to the body its necessary fuel. It is also rich in mineral salts and contains several of the most important vitamins.

Manufacturing Milk Chocolate. Milk chocolate is a combination of chocolate, whole milk solids, sugar, and cocoa butter. Pure granulated sugar and fresh creamy whole milk are first combined in large condensing kettles where most of the water in the milk is removed. The resulting taffylike mass is placed in mixers with chocolate liquor from the milling machines. Here the mass turns to a powder, but with the addition of cocoa butter becomes a semifluid paste. Steel roll refiners are used to further smooth and refine the chocolate paste. The final smoothing and flavor-developing operation takes place in large machines equipped with granite rollers under which the chocolate passes continuously for 96 hours, finally acquiring its desired velvety texture and delicate flavor. (Taken from "Chocolate and Cocoa—Nourishing Foods" circa late 1930s.)

Molding Chocolate Bars. Special machinery that monitors the temperature of the chocolate ensures a glossy appearance, proper body, a rich color, and fine texture, all of which are indicative of high-quality chocolate. Molded bars are delivered to wrapping machines where, under the most modern sanitary methods, they are wrapped and protected, and placed in special containers that are completely sealed. The boxed chocolate is kept in thermostatically controlled stockrooms in which the temperature and humidity do not vary throughout the year.

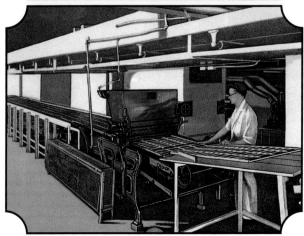

Educational Exhibit of Chocolate and Cocoa circa 1948. Like its educational companion, "Chocolate and Cocoa—Nourishing Foods," this exhibit and accompanying literature has been reprinted numerous times by Hershey. Each edition includes a booklet entitled "The Story of Chocolate and Cocoa," nutritional information on chocolate and cocoa, and several containers of product examples used in the chocolate-manufacturing process. This particular edition contains six glass bottles containing, in order, sample cocoa beans, nibs, shells, chocolate liquor, cocoa butter, and cocoa powder.

"The Story of Chocolate and Cocoa." The 1948 edition of the booklet is liberally illustrated and tells the story of the chocolate-manufacturing process. It also includes contextual information on the Hershey Industrial School and the community of Hershey. The back cover is a picture of the famous HERSHEY COCOA clock, which graces the Chocolate Avenue side of the Windowless Office Building of the Hershey Chocolate Corporation, completed in 1935.

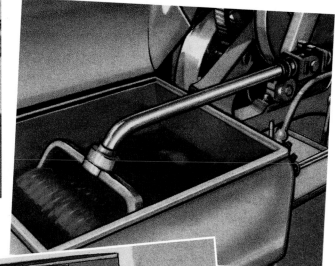

Illustrations from "The Story of Chocolate and Cocoa." This 1938 version of the booklet contains much of the same information and illustrations as its 1948 counterpart.

Experts' Opinions on the Food Value of Chocolate and Cocoa

EDITH C. Williams, Director of the American Food Journal Institute, says that chocolate and cocoa are foods which have gained a rightful place in the diet. As their composition shows, they contain minerals, proteins, fats and carbohydrates, thus supplying four of the essentials. When chocolate and cocoa are combined, as they are with milk, we have a particularly nourishing food which builds bone, gives energy, and builds tissue.

It can be readily seen that as children grow and build bone, they build faster than adults and they need more protein and less energy than the grown-ups. Children need milk, as milk contains valuable minerals for bone-building. If chocolate or cocoa is added to milk, to make it an attractive beverage, the children receive an energy, heat-giving, muscle-building and bone-building food.

CAROLINE B. King, one of America's dietitians, says: "Aside from the delicacy and richness of flavor, cocoa contains qualities which at once recommend it strongly to the dietitian. Because of its comparatively small fat content it is easily digested and is therefore an excellent food for children. Cocoa is especially recommended for the child who must be encouraged to take milk, for it will usually drink its proper quota if cocoa is added in correct proportion. For the invalid and persons of delicate digestion cocoa is one of the most nourishing and easily assimilated of products, and when milk is added it becomes an almost perfect food. In cookery, cocoa is a most prized product. It is convenient, is easily added to other ingredients and adds an exquisite quality and toothsomeness to cakes and desserts. By adding cocoa to a great number of recipes, it improves them immeasurably."

Table of Food Values

		Calories
1 lb. HERSHEY'S Milk Chocolate		2515
1 lb. " Sweet Coating		2465
1 lb. " Almond Chocolate...		2615
1 lb. " Breakfast Cocoa		2035
1 Cup " Cocoa		190
1 Cup Coffee with Cream & Sugar		50
1 Cup Tea		Little if any
1 lb. Lean Beef		880
1 lb. White Fish		680
1 lb. Oysters		235
1 lb. Beets		205
1 lb. Potatoes		325
1 lb. White Bread		1200
1 lb. Apples		285
1 Dozen Eggs		945

HERSHEY CHOCOLATE CORPORATION
19 EAST CHOCOLATE AVENUE
HERSHEY, PA.

Supplement from Educational Exhibit of Chocolate and Cocoa circa 1948. A two-sided insert paid homage to the nutritional value of chocolate and cocoa and included testimonials from two experts.

"The Gift of Montezuma" circa 1972. This educational display poster was published by the Hershey Foods Corporation, Hershey Chocolate and Confectionery Division, as an updated version of its "Chocolate and Cocoa—Nourishing Foods" poster. Printed on simple paper stock, it too was intended to be used as a classroom teaching aid, alone or in conjunction with an updated educational kit and an updated version of the "Story of Chocolate and Cocoa" booklet.

Educational Kit of Chocolate and Cocoa circa 1972. The educational exhibit is now a "kit" and "The Story of Chocolate and Cocoa" now contains updated and enhanced graphics, information on recent corporate acquisitions, the soon-to-be-completed *Hershey's Chocolate World, Hersheypark,* and visitor accommodations. The six containers of chocolate product and by-product are now sealed in plastic and cardboard display boxes.

Cocoa Tin 1978–1987. This back panel from *Hershey's* instant cocoa mix, a powdered drink additive, highlighted the history of chocolate and cocoa.

Cocoa Bean Bag, Hummingbird-Hershey Ltd. circa 1990. Cocoa beans grow only in the tropics, thriving best in a narrow band extending around the world between 10 degrees north and 10 degrees south of the equator. The proximity of the bean to the equator determines the degree of vegetable fat (cocoa butter) in the bean and affects its overall taste. Like other manufacturers, Hershey uses a variety of beans grown in different countries to produce a unique blend and taste for each of its products. Hershey's largest suppliers include the African nations of Ghana, the Ivory Coast, and Nigeria; the South American countries of Ecuador, Brazil, and Venezuela; and the Asian nations of Malaysia and Papua New Guinea.

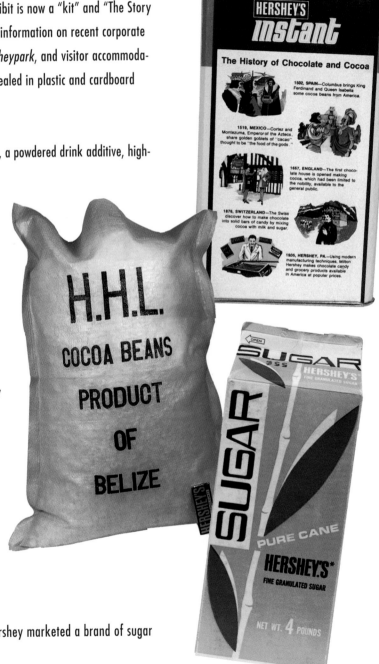

On February 20, 1979, Hershey Foods Corporation announced the purchase of a cocoa bean plantation in Belize, Central America, and named it Hummingbird-Hershey Ltd. Hershey subsequently sold the property in December 1992. It was developed as an educational site to practice modern and innovative methods of growing cocoa.

Hershey's Fine Granulated Sugar 1968–1977. For a short period, Hershey marketed a brand of sugar to consumers.

Cocoa Butter Soaps 1938–1970. For shaving, bathing, or washing, Hershey's various soaps came in a variety of forms, packages, and types over the years.

Metal Molds Used to Form Hershey's Chocolate 1900–1935. Molds used by Milton Hershey in Lancaster and in Hershey were simple flat molds, constructed of iron or nickel and plated with tin, and decorated with the reverse impression of the chocolate to be formed.

Reflecting their European inspiration, most of the Lancaster molds were made in Europe. The round mold on the right side was made by Letang Fils of Paris, France—the oldest existing manufacturer of molds in the world. Later molds were also manufactured throughout Europe as well as in the United States, including a substantial number by Eppelsheimer & Co., the largest manufacturer of chocolate and ice cream molds in this country,

or by jobbers who did not mark their work. Today's molds are often composed of highly specialized plastics, capable of handling extreme production speeds and the rigors of modern manufacturing processes.

Block Mold. This is a modern 10-pound mold used to make solid blocks of chocolate for internal use or for shipment to outside manufacturers to use in coating candies and confections.

Hershey's Milk Chocolate with Almonds Mold circa 1963. This 35-count mold measures 14 $\frac{3}{8}$″ by 28 $\frac{7}{8}$″ and is typical of a production-sized mold.

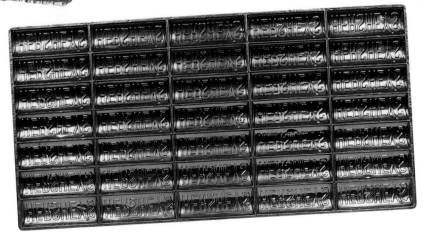

Molds circa 1930-1960. Hershey's milk chocolate bar molds, various sizes.

76

Mold circa 1900. This Hershey Lancaster mold was used in the production of *Hershey's* No. 1 Baking Chocolate.

Large Bar Mold circa 1960. This six-count large-bar mold measures 29 ½" by 8 ½" and was manufactured by B.V. Vormenfabriek, Tilberg, Holland, specifically for the Hershey Chocolate Corporation.

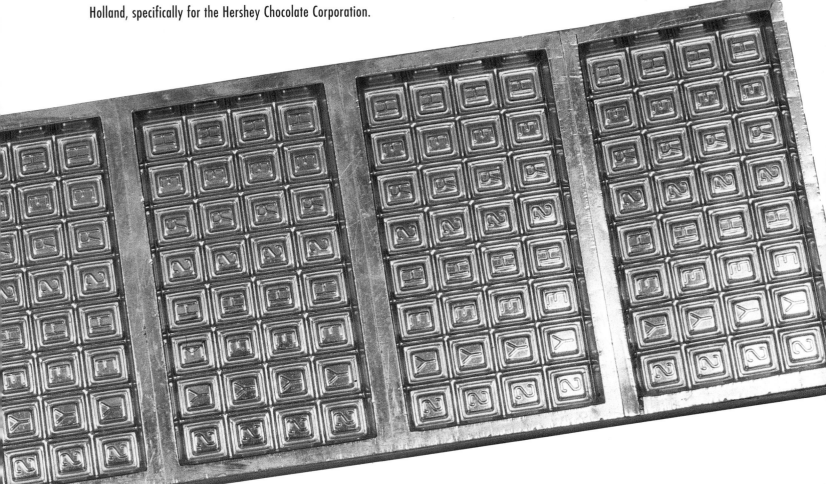

Chapter 4

Coming Home
A New Factory in a Familiar Place

Building the Hershey Chocolate Factory 1903. Ground was broken for the new factory on March 2, 1903. About 50 workers were employed to dig the foundations. Note the abundance of rocks in the field that would become the largest chocolate factory in the world.

THE FACTORY IN A CORNFIELD

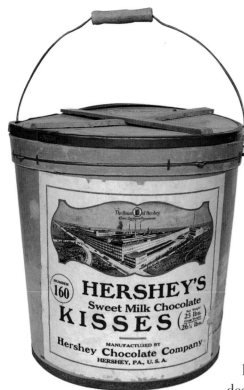

***Hershey's Kisses** Bucket 1920–1927. Hershey used these round containers made of "pulp board" to ship bulk amounts of Hershey's Kisses chocolates.*

To accommodate his new milk chocolate process, Milton Hershey began to construct what would become the world's largest chocolate factory. On a blustery day in March 1903, Milton Hershey found himself standing on a sloping hillside just outside the small village of Derry Church in Derry Township, Dauphin County. Here amidst horses, mules, and wagons, he watched his workmen tear away the earth with shovels and pickaxes to break ground for a factory and a community that in time would capture the imagination of the entire nation. As it turned out, there were more rocks than corn in the five-acre field selected for the factory site. But, ever resourceful, Hershey had them hauled away and used in the construction of the factory and buildings of the town.

In his own experiments, Milton Hershey successfully applied the concepts of mass production to his milk chocolate process; that is, he selected a very limited number of items, froze the design for each, and then manufactured his product in such quantities that the cost to produce each unit decreased as overall volume increased. Initially, he mass-produced only *Hershey's* milk chocolate and *Hershey's* breakfast cocoa. In 1907, he added *Hershey's Kisses* chocolates to the product line and, in 1908, *Hershey's* milk chocolate bar with almonds. In order to reach as many customers as possible, Hershey packaged his candy to sell in one-, two-, and five-cent units in grocery stores, newsstands, and vending machines. This was an important innovation in marketing candy.

After he chose the site for the new factory, Milton Hershey selected C. Emlen Urban, a noted architect from Lancaster responsible for the design of many buildings in that town as well as those to be constructed in Hershey, to design his new factory. The one-story design of the original building reflected Milton Hershey's fear that a multistoried building and its necessary stairways could prove dangerous to employees in case of fire. In June 1905, chocolate production began in Milton Hershey's new factory. Although the new factory was devoted to the manufacture of milk chocolate, Hershey continued to produce sweet chocolate novelties and fancy goods in Lancaster, the Homestead, and the new factory for several years.

HERSHEY'S KISSES CHOCOLATES

The immediate success of *Hershey's* milk chocolate led to the first expansion of the product line in 1907 when the company began to produce *Hershey's Kisses* chocolates. No one knows for sure exactly why Mr. Hershey chose to name his new product *Hershey's Kisses*. One popular theory has the candy named for the sound or motion of the tempered chocolate being deposited on continuous belts during the manufacturing process. Whatever the reason, the size and shape of the standard *Hershey's Kisses* chocolate has remained essentially the same since its introduction in 1907, although there have been a few variations in production methods and packaging over the years. Since their inception, *Hershey's Kisses* have always had a plain flat base and conical shape. It is this shape that allows them to be easily mass-produced on a smooth flat surface. The first *Hershey's Kisses* were also individually hand-wrapped in plain squares of foil. With the advent of the mechanical wrapping machine in 1921, *Hershey's Kisses* could be wrapped much faster using a foil wrap. Always aware of the importance of linking his name with his product, Mr. Hershey used the technology of these machines to add the now-familiar "plume" or "flag" to his product. In 1923, Hershey Chocolate Company obtained a trademark registration for the representation of a "plume" extending out of the wrapper of a candy.

Milton Hershey's first conically shaped chocolate confection was not *Kisses*, but a vanilla sweet chocolate product called *Sweethearts*, which he manufactured between 1900 and 1918. Between 1918 and 1929, Hershey also manufactured a second conical product called *Silverpoints*, which was made with a milk chocolate paste containing more milk than the standard *Hershey's* chocolate.

From 1907 until 1921, *Hershey's Kisses* included a square of tissue that identified each *Kisses* chocolate. Since the tissue was not visible until a *Hershey's Kisses* chocolate was unwrapped, imitators were plentiful. In 1921, Hershey began machine-wrapping *Kisses* with the visible trademark plume that assured consumers they were buying genuine *Hershey's Kisses* before they took a single bite.

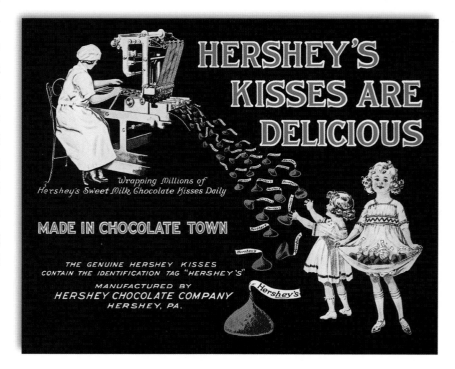

HERSHEY'S HUGS 'N KISSES

This is one of the most endearing *Hershey's* product images of the 1930s, and has been reproduced countless times by Hershey on modern souvenirs and commemorative objects.

Even though the size and shape of the standard *Hershey's Kisses* chocolate has barely changed since its introduction, there have been a number of variations in its composition and packaging. From 1909 until 1931, individually wrapped cone-shaped chocolates were sold under the name *Silvertops*. From 1942 through 1949, the chocolates were not produced because of the rationing of silver foil during and after World War II. *Kisses* were wrapped in colors other than silver for the first time in 1962 when red and green wrappers (in addition to the traditional silver ones) were made available during the Christmas season. Today, *Hershey's Kisses* chocolates are "dressed up" for a number of seasonal occasions. During Easter, the product is available in pastel pink, blue, and green foil. For Valentine's Day, red and silver colors are used. In the fall, brown, gold, and russet colors are made available. The first major reformulation of *Hershey's Kisses* chocolates occurred in September 1990 with the introduction of *Hershey's Kisses with Almonds*, a product containing half an almond and wrapped in gold foil. In the fall of 1993, Hershey introduced *Hershey's Hugs* chocolates and *Hershey's Hugs with Almonds*, conically shaped confections "hugged" with white chocolate.

TIMES OF TRIAL

Between 1910 and 1925, the factory was under almost constant expansion to meet the ever-growing demand of consumers. Various additions to the factory had increased its floor space to a total of 18 acres by 1911 and 35 acres by 1915. The gross revenues of the company had increased more than fivefold from $10.3 million in 1915 to $58 million in 1919. Hershey introduced a number of new chocolate products, including *Mr. Goodbar* in November 1925 and *Hershey's* cocoa syrup, a forerunner of *Hershey's* syrup, in January 1926. Despite these successes, two significant problems also confronted Milton Hershey during this period. The first problem was a direct result of World War I. With the outbreak of war in Europe in 1914, sugar became scarce. At that time, the sugar used in the manufacture of chocolate was not cane sugar, but beet sugar obtained from beet fields in Europe. As the war in Europe continued, Hershey looked to Cuba as a more secure source for sugar. In May 1916, Hershey began to acquire

*Hand Packing and Weighing **Kisses** Chocolates circa Early 1930s. Factory employees manually weigh 2 1/2-pound boxes of Hershey's Kisses chocolates.*

Hershey's Kisses Valentine's Day
Advertisements 1988–1990.

Hershey's Kisses Easter Advertisement circa 1990.

Hershey's Hugs Advertisements 1993. It took several years and special advancements in technology for Hershey Chocolate to produce *Hugs* candy. *Hugs* are miniature *Hershey's Kisses* "hugged" by white chocolate. *Hugs* are the first successful *Hershey's* product to use white chocolate.

HAPPY EASTER FROM HERSHEY'S KISSES.

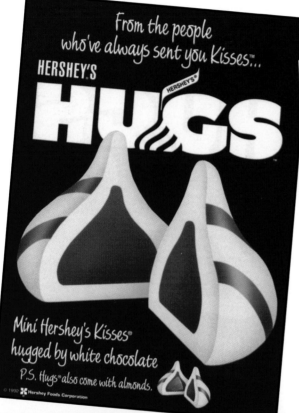

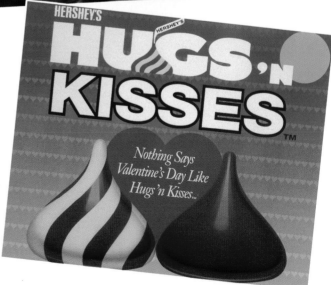

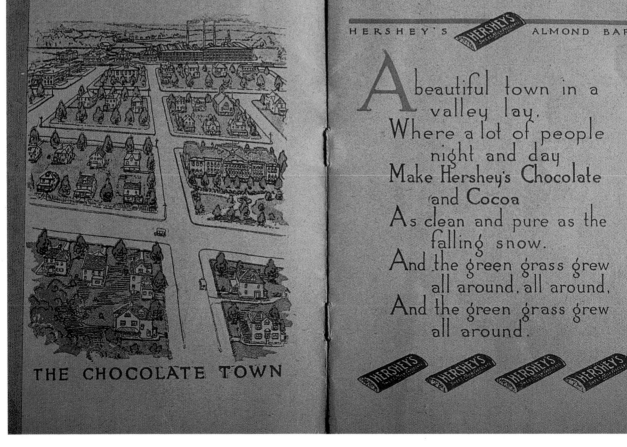

Hershey's Green Grass Jingle Book
for Little Folks circa 1915.

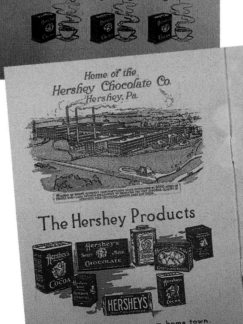

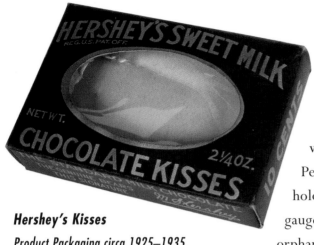

Hershey's Kisses

Product Packaging circa 1925–1935. Hershey's Kisses chocolates appeared in a variety of packages in the 1920s and '30s. Packaging produced before 1927 (above) is marked as being a product of the Hershey Chocolate Company and contains the words SWEET MILK CHOCOLATE. *Those produced between 1928 and 1932 (right) are still labeled as* SWEET MILK CHOCOLATE, *but are marked as a product of the Hershey Chocolate Corporation. Packaging manufactured beginning in 1933 (below) is simply marked* MILK CHOCOLATE *and is also marked as a product of the Hershey Chocolate Corporation. This designation remained as such until the company reorganized itself as the Hershey Foods Corporation in 1968.*

Cuban sugar-cane plantations and mills, eventually establishing a sugar refinery and town known as Central Hershey; "central" being the name for a sugar processing plant and its support facilities in Cuba. The Cuban town was a planned community, inspired by its central Pennsylvania namesake. At its height, the Hershey Cuban holdings included 60,000 acres, five sugar mills, a standard gauge railroad with 251 miles of track, and even a school for orphaned children. In 1946, the Hershey sugar and railway interests in Cuba were sold to the Cuban-Atlantic Sugar Company.

With his chocolate company growing, Milton Hershey took steps to ensure that his supply of sugar would not be interrupted by events in Europe during World War I. He decided to make a move—and with that move came the company's first major setback. Milton Hershey felt that until his Cuban mills could meet the demand of his factory, large quantities of sugar would need to be purchased to keep adequate reserves on hand. Buying on margin, he accumulated his sugar reserves. Unfortunately, with the end of the war, the sugar market collapsed. Sugar that Milton

Hershey had bought on margin at 26 $1/2$ cents came in at $1^1/_2$ cents. The deficit created by this collapse resulted in a bottom-line loss of $1,109,000 for the chocolate company in 1920. When compared with the company's 1919 profit of $6 million, the turnaround was catastrophic. Milton Hershey was forced to borrow money to cover his losses. He approached the National City Bank of New York, which agreed to float a bond issue of $20 million, taking a mortgage on the Hershey properties until the debt could be paid. As part of the deal, the bank appointed a "watchdog" representative for both the Pennsylvania and Cuban properties. Motivated in part by Milton Hershey's frustration over the conditions of the loan, the company paid back its obligation to National City Bank in June of 1922. Milton Hershey was once again at the helm of his company.

Hershey's Kisses Easter Boxes. (Clockwise) 1930–1933; 1938–1939; 1949; 1951–1952.

With the end of World War I, Milton Hershey had to face two separate threats to the very existence of his chocolate company: the collapse of the world sugar market in 1920 and an unexpected fallout from the onset of Prohibition. With Prohibition established as the law of the land by the 18th Amendment to the U.S. Constitution, the Schlitz Brewing Company of Milwaukee found itself in danger of being legislated out of business. In response, the company decided to create the Eline Chocolate Company and enter the confectionery business. They recruited a number of talented Hershey employees and used their expertise to build a manufacturing plant in Milwaukee that was very similar to the Hershey plant. The Eline brand failed to entice consumers and Schlitz soon abandoned the project. Because Milton Hershey valued loyalty above all else, those who left the Hershey organization were never welcomed back. The episode proved to Milton Hershey and to the country that, despite the loss of some of his top talent, he and his product were here to stay.

Hershey's Kisses Holiday Bands.
Holiday bands such as this were
wrapped around cellophane packages
of *Kisses* to promote sales on Easter
(1937–1939), Valentine's Day
(1956), and other holidays.

SIX STICKS FOR A NICKEL

In May 1915, Milton Hershey began to manufacture chewing gum. Unlike his enterprises in chocolate and sugar, this concern was not motivated solely by his desire to produce a quality confection, but in large part to settle a personal grudge with the manufacturer of Wrigley's Gum. This was not the first time Hershey and Wrigley had crossed paths. Knowing the pride Wrigley took in his Chicago Cubs baseball team, Milton Hershey had previously attempted to purchase the Philadelphia Nationals (who later became the Philadelphia Phillies) and move the team to Hershey. With that failure, Hershey turned to manufacturing *Easy Chew* mint-flavored chewing gum in an effort to challenge Wrigley at his own game.

Although manufactured by Hershey, *Easy Chew* chewing gum first appeared under the Easy Chew Gum Company name so as to not reflect poorly on the *Hershey's* name should the product fail. It was Hershey's long-time business associate, Mr. William Murrie, who came up with the idea of giving the public a bonus sixth stick in every pack as opposed to the industry standard of five per pack. The product was an immediate hit and *Easy Chew* became a product of *Hershey Chewing Gum*. Milton Hershey's success with a gum product was short-lived, in view of stiff competition from Wrigley's. Also, because of his speculation in sugar and import restrictions on the commodity after World War I, Hershey had trouble supplying both his chocolate and gum product lines with sugar in the early 1920s. Hershey discontinued production of *Easy Chew* gum in October 1924.

Have You Tried
HERSHEY'S Chewing Gum?
Six Sticks for 5¢

Hershey's Chewing Gum 1915–1924. Few people realize that the Hershey Chocolate Company once manufactured a mint-flavored chewing gum. Hershey packaged his gum six sticks to a pack, 20 packs to a box. However, after some initial success, sales never reached a level to make continued production profitable.

Door Pull circa 1920s. Even door handles and door pulls in the new factory displayed the "Baby-in-the-Bean" corporate logo.

After eighty years of making Kisses,™

HERSHEY'S®

WE FINALLY WENT NUTS.

Introducing HERSHEY'S KISSES® WITH ALMONDS

Hershey's Kisses with Almonds Advertisement 1990. To mark the introduction of *Hershey's Kisses with Almonds* in September 1990, a 500-pound gold-colored replica of the product was dropped from the flagpole atop One Times Square—the same place from which the ball marking the beginning of each new year is dropped.

Silverpoints 1918–1929. Because *Silverpoints* utilized a different milk chocolate recipe, they were not marketed under the *Hershey's* name, but instead appeared as a product of a Hershey subsidiary—The Chocolate Sales Corporation.

HOMESTEAD MILK CHOCOLATE

Silverpoints 5 for 1c

CHOCOLATE SALES CORPORATION
HERSHEY, PA.

ITEM NO. 242 Homestead MILK CHOCOLATE Silverpoints 750 COUNT
MANUFACTURED BY HERSHEY CHOCOLATE CORPORATION, HERSHEY, PA., U.S.A.

ITEM NO. 241 HOMESTEAD MILK CHOCOLATE Silverpoints 375 COUNT
MANUFACTURED BY HERSHEY CHOCOLATE CORPORATION, HERSHEY, PA., U.S.A.

No. 130 HERSHEY'S MILK CHOCOLATE KISSES 2½ lbs.
MANUFACTURED BY HERSHEY CHOCOLATE CORPORATION, HERSHEY, PA.U.S.A.

No. 140 HERSHEY'S REG. U.S. PAT. OFF. MILK CHOCOLATE KISSES 5 lbs.
MANUFACTURED BY HERSHEY CHOCOLATE CORPORATION, HERSHEY, PA., U.S.A.

HERSHEYS MILK CHOCOLATE Made with fresh milk!

MORE SUSTAINING THAN MEAT

HERSHEY'S SWEET MILK CHOCOLATE

NET WEIGHT QUARTER POUND

THE GENUINE BEARS THIS SIGNATURE *M.S.Hershey*

ALMOND HERSHEY'S SWEET MILK CHOCOLATE

Chocolate Bars 1915–1920. The labels for milk chocolate bars changed many times during the early years of the Hershey Chocolate Company. Once the ink was gold, not silver. Several different borders were also used over the years. Slogans such as "More Sustaining Than Meat" and "The Genuine Bears This Signature" were important design elements until 1930.

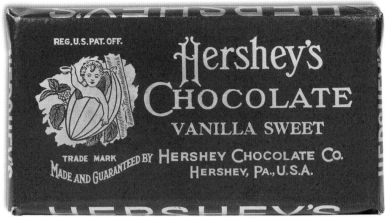

Hershey's *Vanilla Sweet Chocolate.* Baking chocolate flavored with vanillin from (above) 1905–1927, $\frac{1}{2}$-lb. size, and (right) 1927.

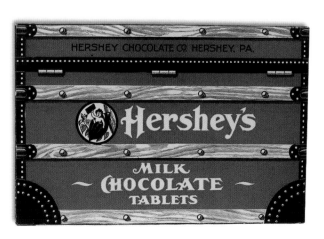

Hershey's *Product Packages 1905–1920.* During his early years in Hershey, Milton Hershey continued to market a small number of milk chocolate products in fancy packages.

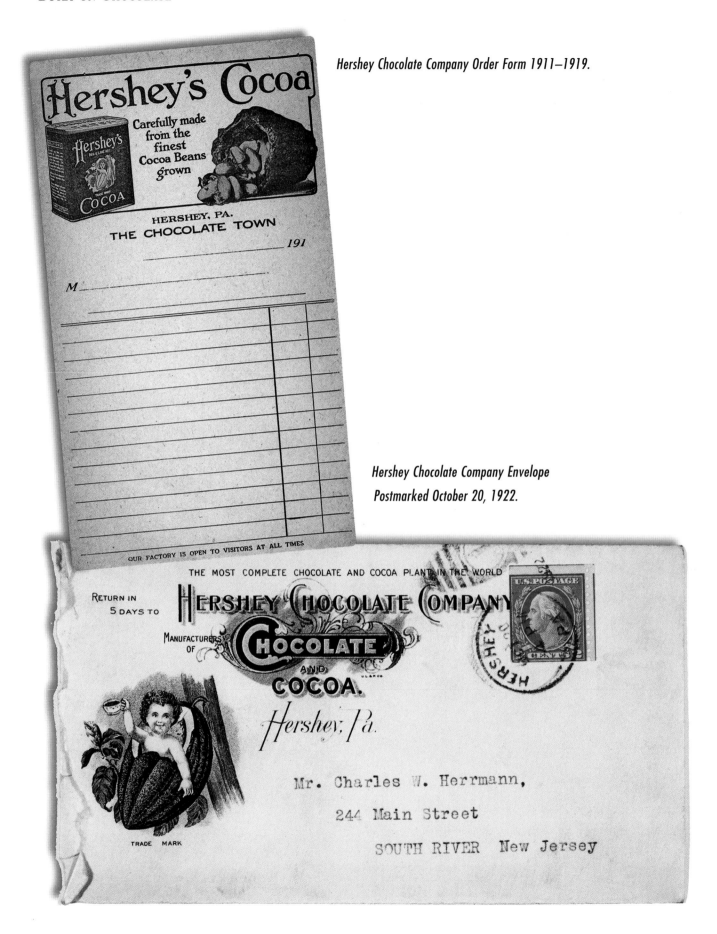

Hershey Chocolate Company Order Form 1911–1919.

Hershey Chocolate Company Envelope
Postmarked October 20, 1922.

Hershey's *Cocoa Tin Label 1924–1928.* This printed tin "blank" was used to form the half-pound tin.

Hershey's Homestead *Chocolate Bars 1926.* These bars were manufactured by the Hershey Chocolate Company using a different milk chocolate formula than that used for standard production bars.

Images from the Salespersons' Sample Booklet circa 1915. Most of Milton Hershey's production by 1915 was in milk chocolate, baking chocolate, and cocoa, which appeared in a standardized silver and maroon label—similar to that which we know today. Although he continued to market and develop new products and product packaging, product recognition (through a standardized appearance in packaging) was now an

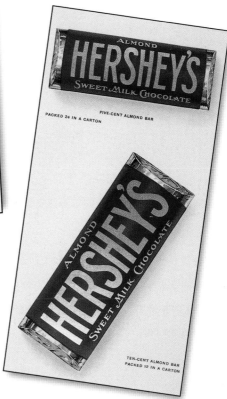

important element of Hershey's overall selling strategy.

In 1915, chocolate bars were offered for retail sale at 10, 5, 3, and 2 cents and almond bars at 10 and 5 cents. *Kisses* chocolates sold for 10 cents and also came in 2 $1/2$- or 5-pound cartons. Baking chocolate came in $1/4$- and $1/2$- pound cartons and cocoa in $1/5$-, $1/4$-, $1/2$-, 1-, or 5-lb. tins.

Club Cocoa circa 1915. While Hershey Chocolate is famous for its variety of confectionery products, it is not as well known that until the 1950s, Hershey also maintained a substantial business in bulk chocolate. *Club Cocoa* was one of more than 15 grades of cocoa Hershey produced for commercial use. In addition, Hershey also manufactured a wide assortment of coating chocolate for other confectioners.

Hershey's Cocoa Advertisement circa 1920.

The Hershey Girl 1916. The company experimented with advertising locally during the early years of business in Hershey. "The Hershey Girl" was a factory employee and the image appeared in the local paper. As a rule, the company did not advertise its products through the media until 1970.

Advertising Leaflet 1906–1910. Company salesmen used leaflets such as this to promote the sale of *Hershey's* chocolate.

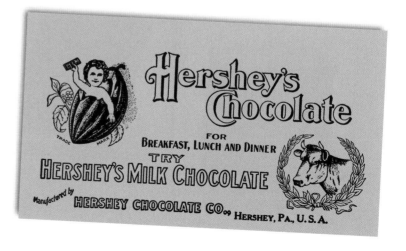

When introduced in 1900, *Hershey's* milk chocolate was promoted as a healthful, wholesome treat. Advertising illustrations such as this one from around 1910 highlighted milk chocolate's ties to fresh milk and country pastures.

"A Meal in Itself" 1920–1924. Since the conquest of the Aztecs by the Spanish Conquistadors in the early 1500s, chocolate has been touted as a wonder food. Into the 20th century, nutritionists recommended chocolate and cocoa as part of a balanced nutritional diet. Hershey and other manufacturers emphasized the benefits of their chocolate products in their promotions as well.

The use of children to advertise products is not a recent phenomenon. Placards such as this were found in grocery stores and candy counters throughout America in the early years of the 20th century.

The *Hershey's* milk chocolate bar with almonds was introduced in 1908. Hershey's demand for almonds grew so great that in 1965 the company began buying land to develop almond groves in California. Before it was sold in 1977, Hershey owned over 5,000 acres of almond orchards.

Easy Desserts Advertisement circa 1920. Until 1970, Hershey advertised its products to consumers primarily through point-of-purchase displays such as this one. Since the early 1900s, Hershey has also relied upon retail window displays to entice consumers, and has offered a variety of cookbooks to help consumers find new ways to use its products.

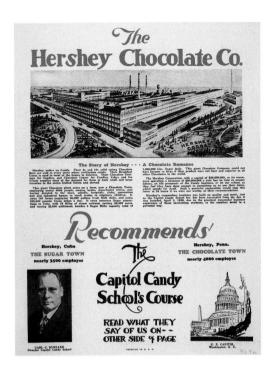

Homemade Candy for Profit—The Capitol Candy School's Correspondence Course 1928. During the 1920s, home study vocational courses were all the rage. This particular course claimed that "spare-time home Kitchen study at start usually develops into Own dainty Candy Shop" and presented a "wonderful new occupation for women." William Murrie, president of Hershey Chocolate Corporation, in a letter dated November 20, 1928, personally recommended the 20-lesson course. Murrie wrote, "We recall the pleasant relationship which existed between your House and our own…. Based upon your personal experience of 30 years in the candy business we believe that you are in excellent position to instruct persons desiring to learn how to manufacture candy."

Hershey's Cocoa 1920–1927. By the late 1920s, Hershey produced some 50,000 pounds of cocoa each day.

Mr. Goodbar Poster circa 1925. Introduced in 1925, the *Mr. Goodbar* chocolate bar combines milk chocolate and peanuts. According to popular legend, Milton Hershey himself named the bar. When taste-testing the new confection, Mr. Hershey is said to have exclaimed, "Now, that's a Goodbar!"

In an attempt to provide another outlet for marketing and advertising *Hershey's* chocolate, vending machines were placed in various mass-transit depots and other high-traffic public areas throughout the country. They became an effective form of distribution and advertising during the 1920s and remained in use until after World War II.

"MADE ON THE FARM"

OUR LOCATION HELPS VERY MUCH IN PRODUCING THAT SUPERIOR RICH FLAVOR IN HERSHEY'S MILK CHOCOLATE AND ALMOND BARS HERSHEY CHOCOLATE CO. HERSHEY, PA.

MILKING TIME
require 5000 cows to supply us with mil

HERSHEY CHOCOLATE CO. HERSHEY, PA. HERSHEY'S ALMOND BARS AND MILK CHOCOLATE ARE RICH WITH PURE COUNTRY MILK WE DO ALL OUR MILKING WITH SANITARY MILKING MACHINES

One of the many herds, Hershey Chocolate Co. Hershey, Pa.

A SECTION OF ONE OF THE FINISHING ROOMS
Hershey Chocolate Co., Hershey, Pa.

HERSHEY INN
APARTMENTS FOR SOME OF OUR EMPLOYES
Hershey Chocolate Co., Hershey, Pa.

1909–1918. Much like he did in Lancaster, Milton Hershey continued to place bar cards in his milk chocolate bars in Hershey. However, instead of using fanciful collector cards, Hershey used actual

ATHLETIC FIELD – HERSHEY, PA.
Home of the Hershey Chocolate Co.

CHILDREN'S PLAYGROUNDS – HERSHEY, PA.
Home of the Hershey Chocolate Co.

VIEW OF THE SWATARA, NEAR HERSHEY, PA.

A Recreation Spot,
Hershey Chocolate Co.,
Hershey, Pa.

Hershey Park Rustic Bridge,
Hershey Chocolate Co.,
Hershey, Pa.

photographs (either black-and-white, green-toned, or colored) printed on the front of postcards to advertise the fresh, wholesome ingredients of his product; the sanitary nature of his chocolate-making process; and the beauty of the model community of Hershey and its environs. When mailed, the postcards were an effective form of advertisement.

~ MADE ON THE FARM ~

This
Illustrates a real Cocoa pod right from the plantation, broken open, showing
the natural Cocoa beans as used by the Hershey Chocolate Co., Hershey, P

1909–1918. To emphasize the wholesomeness of the product, "Made on the Farm" became a hallmark of Hershey's advertising efforts.

Cocoa Recipes Mail Promotion 1909–1918. Hershey found the U.S. Postal Service a useful tool in reaching consumers. Bar cards, mailed to friends and relatives, provided an effective means to promote his product and the town of Hershey throughout the United States. Hershey also encouraged consumers to use his cocoa by offering easily obtainable recipes promptly delivered through the mail system.

Hershey's bar cards did indeed travel throughout the United States. This postcard was sent on April 25, 1915, from Phoenix, Arizona, to Greencastle, Indiana, and reads in part, "you can see that I have had more candy as I always remember you with the cards…"

View of the Hershey Chocolate Factory circa 1910. This card is postmarked June 20, 1910, and provides an interesting bird's-eye view of the factory complex only five years after completion of the first factory building in June 1905.

View of the Hershey Chocolate Factory circa 1912. These were years of explosive growth for the chocolate company in terms of sales and floor space. Between 1910 and 1912, for example, the factory had already greatly increased in size and would continue to do so until the mid-1920s.

The Recently Completed Hershey Chocolate Factory and Its Founder in the Winter of 1905.

The Home of Hershey's circa 1915. This point-of-purchase retail display poster was placed in storefront windows with various *Hershey's* products to attract customers. This was reproduced from the original watercolor artwork.

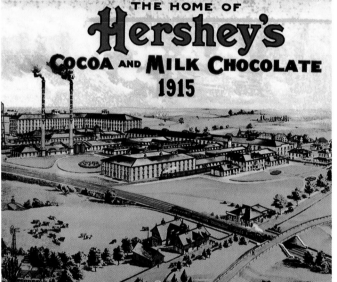

(Left) This box top is a close-up of the factory taken from the original watercolor. It is an unusual *Hershey's* product image in that it prominently displays a date.

(Below, left) *Hershey Chocolate Company and Railroad Station circa 1920.* The printed description on the reverse of this hand-colored postcard reads, "The chocolate and cocoa factory is of daylight construction, with unusual efficiency details. It has more than 45 acres of floor space and is fronted and flanked by beautiful parks and all around it are wide open spaces."

(Below) *New Factory Addition circa 1920.* This addition is to the east end of the factory. Maroon barberry bushes in the foreground spelling HERSHEY COCOA can still be seen at the site today.

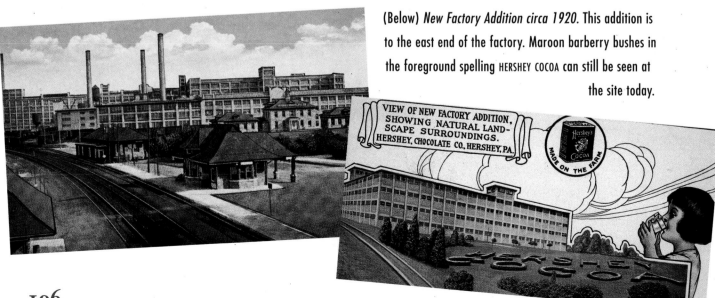

Sweet Chocolate Coating Bag 1925–1935. In Lancaster, supplying outside manufacturers with sweet chocolate coatings was an important aspect of the chocolate-making business. In Hershey, the production of sweet chocolate coatings and related products became less important as time proved the profitability of milk chocolate. By 1920, Hershey had established the Chocolate Sales Corporation to handle less-profitable areas of production. Hershey used bags like these to ship solid blocks of sweet chocolate coatings to outside manufacturers.

Mold 1925–1935. This 10-pound, tinned-iron mold was used to form sweet chocolate blocks for shipping by the Chocolate Sales Corporation.

Hershey's Pure Cane Sugar, Five-Pound Size 1928–1946. Hershey produced sugar in Cuba for both wholesale and retail sale. Cotton bags of processed sugar came in weights up to 100 pounds or down to 5 pounds. The Hershey Corporation was created in 1927 to specifically manage all aspects of the Cuban operation. In 1946, the Hershey holdings—including sugar, railroad, hemp, and sunflower oil interests in Cuba—were sold to the Cuban-Atlantic Sugar Company.

Milk Chocolate Coating Bag 1930–1940. Hershey produced 10-pound blocks of milk chocolate coatings for outside jobbers for many years. This bag was used to wrap and ship each individual block.

The Great Smokestacks of the Hershey Cuban Sugar Mill circa 1930–1935. Milton Hershey's first business experiences in Philadelphia and New York had taught him a number of valuable lessons which he would successfully apply to his later business endeavors. One was the necessity of controlling the supply of raw materials—especially sugar—in the manufacture of confectionery products. However, Hershey's single-minded approach to this ideal would have disastrous consequences for him in the post–World War I collapse of the sugar market.

A GLOBAL MARKET

During World War I, chocolate itself was mobilized. Emergency rations issued to American soldiers included candy bars. The high sugar content of chocolate made it an excellent source of immediate high energy. However, the problem with chocolate as an emergency ration was its taste: the young American soldiers rarely saved their one-ounce bars for a yet-unforeseen-crisis. Most often a soldier ate his ration right away. The more kindhearted "doughboy" shared his rations with starving local civilians. When these soldiers returned to America at the close of the war, they were hungry for chocolate. Fueled by their taste, chocolate was in demand everywhere and a plethora of companies and a multitude of chocolate bar names quickly entered the market. In 1923, one such entrepreneur was H.B. Reese, a Hershey employee who established his own small factory in the basement of his Hershey home. In 1928, the H.B. Reese Candy Company began to make *Reese's* peanut butter cups. The original peanut butter cup is still around, sold under the same name, although it is now operated as a division of Hershey since its purchase in 1963.

THE COMPANY GOES PUBLIC

In 1927, Milton Hershey decided to refinance and reorganize his company. He incorporated the Hershey Chocolate Company as the Hershey Chocolate Corporation and offered to the public 150,000 shares of common stock. The National City Company handled the arrangements by purchasing the shares for $15.5 million and then reselling the shares to the public. Since stockholders might be inclined to question the wisdom of the company in spending its earnings on items involving the community of Hershey, Milton Hershey grouped his nonchocolate domestic enterprises under another corporate umbrella called Hershey Estates. He also established a third entity called the Hershey Corporation to handle the Cuban operations.

These transactions occurred in an era of grandiose thinking, in a day marked by huge mergers and acquisitions. It was an era characterized by a joining of forces among the great names in industry and commerce who could see tremendous opportunity in developing national distribution systems. Those in high finance stood to gain in the marketing of new securities derived from such ventures and combinations. Yet in such an era, characterized by misleading superficial labels like "The Roaring '20s" and "The Jazz Age," the seeds of financial discontent had already been sown. In two short years, the country would experience "The Crash of 1929" and plunge headlong into the Great Depression, forever changing Hershey and the country at large.

(Opposite, bottom) *Grand Cross of the National Order of Carlos Manuel de Cespedes 1933.* The sugar mill at Central Hershey was completed in 1918 and ground its first sugar cane in January 1919. Very quickly, a town was built around the sugar mill. As the town and mill prospered, Milton Hershey began to buy other sugar districts, including Central San Juan Bautista, Central Rosario, Central Carmen, Central San Antonio, and, finally, in 1927, Central Jesus Maria. At Central Rosario, Milton Hershey built his Cuban Orphan School to educate Cuban children in much the same manner as the Hershey Industrial School. For all his work, Milton Hershey was made an "Adopted Son and Honorary Citizen" of Matanzas in May 1924. It was a few years later, however—on February 1, 1933, to be precise—that Hershey received the greatest honor that Cuba could bestow. At the Presidential Palace in Havana, he was presented with the Grand Cross in recognition for his contribution to the nation's growth and development. In making the award, President Machado noted, "With this medal we give a bit of our soul and with it goes our lasting admiration."

Chapter 5

Hershey, Pennsylvania
Chocolate Town, U.S.A.!

Airplane View with **Hershey Park** *in the Foreground in 1953.*

This is the front cover of the booklet by Joseph Richard Snavely. It was reprinted in 1953 as part of the town's 50th anniversary.

A TOWN TO MEET EVERY NEED

When Milton Hershey chose a rural site for his chocolate factory, he also envisioned building a complete new community. He agreed with industrialists who believed as he did that providing a healthy environment for workers made good business sense. Well aware of what he needed and wanted in his town from the start, Milton Hershey selected Henry Herr, a well-known consulting engineer from Lancaster, to conduct the necessary surveys for the chocolate factory, railroad sidings, streets, houses, water mains, sewage system, trolleys, park, and whatever else it would take to develop the town. Beginning in January 1903, Herr and a corps of surveyors began their work. That same month, a charter was also granted to the Hummelstown and Campbelltown Street Railway Company and in March construction began on the plant itself.

In July, the first telephone line was installed in what was then still Derry Church and the first surveys were made for High Point mansion, Mr. and Mrs. Hershey's home.

PICNIC GETAWAY

In July 1903, Hershey set aside land in the center of town for a future community park to be known as *Hershey Park*. *Hershey Park* opened to the public in the spring of 1907. Picnicking and informal group outings were favorite pastimes in the park during its early years. Special excursion trains and trolleys brought large groups from surrounding communities to enjoy the playground, baseball, band concerts, and canoeing on Spring Creek. In 1908, the park added a merry-go-round as its first major ride. The park continued to expand and to add many new rides in the following decades. Visitors paid an individual fee for each ride until 1972, when *Hershey Park* was rechristened *Hersheypark*, embarked upon a multiphased expansion, and initiated a one-price admission plan. Despite these changes, the park has never lost sight of its commitment to wholesome family entertainment and has retained its clean and green appearance with mature trees and extensive plantings.

A TOWN TAKES SHAPE

When the new factory began to produce milk chocolate in June 1905, many buildings and public works considered to be essential by Milton Hershey were already in place. The most prominent of these buildings was the Cocoa House (which housed a bank, post office, general store, and several boarding rooms) and the McKinley School. Perhaps motivated by his own educational experiences, Milton Hershey worked to create a modern public educational system by consolidating the many one-room schoolhouses of the area and providing for the construction of the McKinley School. He also worked hard to see that his town did not look and sound like other towns. Homes were built in a variety of conventional yet comfortable styles to avoid the uniform housing sometimes found in other planned communities. Hershey encouraged workers to own rather than to rent their homes. In the residential districts, no public or commercial building could be erected. Hershey hired a landscape architect to assist with the landscaping of the entire town. Trees were planted along the street and flower beds were planted in public spaces. The main street on which the factory faced was part of the Berks and Dauphin Counties Turnpike and from the beginning was called Chocolate Avenue. The major intersecting street became Cocoa Avenue. Both the Cocoa House and the McKinley School were located at this intersection, which became the commercial center of the town. The Cocoa House was home to the YMCA for a short period. In 1912, the YMCA became the Hershey

Signpost for One of the Most Famous Intersections in America—Cocoa and Chocolate Avenues circa 1920.

East Chocolate Avenue, Looking East, circa 1920. The McKinley School on the right side of this photograph was originally constructed in 1905 as one of the first buildings in Hershey. In 1910, Hershey expanded the building to accommodate the ever-increasing number of students in the burgeoning town.

Chocolate Avenue, Looking North, 1914. The Hershey Trust Company building on the northwest corner of Chocolate and Cocoa Avenues was completed on July 13, 1914. Over the next several years, a new consolidated school, convention hall, and press building would be completed. In this view, the finishing touches are being placed on the Hershey Press building. In 1920, the press building would become the home of the Hershey Department Store, formerly located across the street on the first floor of the Hershey Inn since 1910.

Men's Club. Soon other streets sprang up with names echoing the countries in which cocoa beans were grown—names like Trinidad, Java, Caracas, Areba, Granada, and Ceylon hosted residential areas. The first homes were built on Trinidad, Cocoa, and Chocolate Avenues. As the town grew in size, the commercial establishments originally located in the Cocoa House moved to their own buildings. First to move were the Hershey Inn and the Hershey Store Company (later the Hershey Department Store) in 1910. In 1914, the Hershey Trust Company moved to its new building.

C. EMLEN URBAN

The physical appearance of Milton Hershey's model town was mostly the work of one man—C. Emlen Urban. Urban was Lancaster, Pennsylvania's most prominent architect at the turn of the century. He designed many commercial buildings and residences in Lancaster, where he became an acquaintance and close personal friend of Milton Hershey's. Urban designed all of Hershey's buildings between 1903 and 1924, including the original chocolate factory buildings and High Point Mansion (Milton Hershey's own home), as well as many of the homes of chocolate-company executives. The Hershey Community Building and Theatre, designed by Urban in 1915 but not constructed until the early 1930s, is arguably the most beautiful building designed by Urban. He died in his Lancaster home in 1939.

NAMING THE TOWN

Milton Hershey's new community grew quickly and with it came the need to establish a post office. The new post office needed a name. Mr. Hershey offered a prize of $100 for the best new name. The public proposed thousands of names until "Hersheykoko" was selected. The U.S. Post Office discouraged the use of this name, finding it too commercial. Finally, the name of "Hershey" was

chosen and on February 7, 1906, the Hershey Post Office received its first mail delivery. To this day, the town remains an unincorporated entity and has no official governmental standing. It is part of the Township of Derry and the schools are part of the Derry Township School District. Hershey is probably one of the few communities in the nation named for its post office!

THE *HERSHEY* TRANSIT COMPANY

Milton Hershey wasted little time in getting his trolleys running. Hershey realized a trolley would provide an economical and convenient way for freight (primarily milk from surrounding dairy farms) and passengers (primarily workers from nearby established towns) to arrive at the new factory. Regular service on the Hummelstown and Campbelltown Street Railway Company began in October 1904. The trolley lines eventually extended to cities throughout central Pennsylvania and from there to major cities in the northeast. By 1915, the extensive system of freight and passenger lines were combined to form the *Hershey* Transit Company. Visitors, residents, workers, and students of the Hershey Industrial School all used the system. However, with increased automobile and truck traffic on an ever-growing system of highways and improved roads, the trolley slowly became obsolete to both passenger and freight traffic. In 1942, freight service ended and on December 21, 1946, the Hershey Trolley made its last regularly scheduled passenger run.

Hershey High School 1908. Milton Hershey was very interested in the education of children. The McKinley School was completed in 1905 as one of the first two buildings completed by Mr. Hershey for his town (the other being the Cocoa House).

HIGH POINT MANSION

In 1903, Milton and Catherine Hershey chose a sight overlooking the chocolate factory for their new home. However, construction of the mansion did not begin until the spring of 1906 and it was not until the spring of 1908 that the building was completed. A large glass torchère purchased by Milton Hershey at the 1893 Colombian Exposition in Chicago dominated the entrance foyer. Catherine Hershey made sure the rooms were full of color. Beautiful gardens dominated the grounds. In comparison to the homes of most millionaires of the time, however, High Point was modest in both size and appointments. It had few rooms, no bar, and no swimming pool. The attending staff was also small. Unfortunately, the Hersheys spent only a few years in the home together. On March 25, 1915, Catherine Hershey died after a long illness. Milton Hershey was devastated by her death and never remarried. He continued to live in High Point until his death in 1945. However, in 1930, he gave his home to the Hershey Country Club for use as a clubhouse, retaining an upstairs "apartment."

IT WAS KITTY'S IDEA

Perhaps as a result of her illness and saddened by their inability to have children, Catherine Hershey urged her husband to establish a school for orphaned boys. On November 15, 1909, the Hersheys created the Hershey Industrial School, now named Milton Hershey School. As a result of his own experiences, Mr. Hershey wanted the school to provide the boys with a stable home life, a sound education, and a trade. The first class consisted of 10 boys. Milton Hershey's birthplace, the Homestead, served as the first home and classroom for the boys. From its beginnings, the school was designed to

The Cocoa House 1905. This two-story building housed a bank, post office, and general store on the first floor. The second floor contained boarding rooms. The building was demolished in 1963 to make way for a new structure housing offices and the Hershey Drug Store.

The Men's Club circa 1915. In 1910, the Cocoa House was renovated to be the home of the YMCA. The Hershey Post Office, along with the Hershey Volunteer Fire Company, had already moved to a new adjacent building located between the Cocoa House and the chocolate factory in 1906. The Hershey Store Company, later the Hershey Department Store, moved to the first floor of the Hershey Inn in 1910. In October 1913, the Hershey Men's Club replaced the YMCA.

provide a homelike environment for the boys. They were grouped by age in homes supervised by housemothers (for younger boys) or married couples serving as house parents (for older boys). Meals were served "family style" and each boy helped in taking care of the home. In 1918, three years after the death of his wife, Milton Hershey placed the bulk of his fortune, $60 million worth of Hershey Chocolate Company stock, in trust for his school. The School Trust was and still is managed by the Hershey Trust Company, which had been established in 1905 to provide the town's financial services. The School Trust ensures the School's continued ability to provide a full education and a secure, nurturing environment for all attending students. Only income and dividends from the School Trust's investments may be used for the benefit of the school. During the 1920s, the school added an agricultural program to its curriculum. Older boys lived in homes connected to farms where they raised turkeys, pigs, ducks, and cows. As enrollment grew, additional buildings, homes, and farmland were added to the school. In 1932, Milton Hershey also contributed to the School Trust his stock in Hershey Estates, today known as the Hershey Entertainment and Resort Company or HERCO. The school's Deed of Trust has been modified four times: in 1933 to change the enrollment age from ages 4 to 8 to ages 4 to 14; in 1950 to change the name to Milton Hershey School; in 1968 to permit the enrollment of minority males; and in 1976 to permit the enrollment of girls.

The Hershey Department Store and Hershey Inn circa 1920. After its completion in 1910, the Hershey Inn occupied the second floor and the Hershey Store Company (later the Hershey Department Store) occupied the first floor. The inn took over the entire building in 1920 when the department store moved across the street to the former press building. Two additional stories were added in 1936 and the building was renamed the Community Inn. In 1958, the entire building was remodeled and renamed the Cocoa Inn.

The Hershey Café circa 1915. This building, adjacent to the chocolate factory, first opened on October 26, 1910, for the use of the chocolate-company employees. A year later, it opened to the general public. It had been originally constructed as a trolley car barn. The building was taken over by the company's sales office before its demolition in 1931 to make way for the Windowless Office Building.

Today, the Milton Hershey School provides a cost-free education and home to over 1,100 underprivileged children in grades kindergarten through 12. Through the School Trust, Milton Hershey School benefits from the financial success of both Hershey Foods Corporation, successor to the Hershey Chocolate Company, and HERCO.

BUILDING UP IN THE FACE OF ADVERSITY

The Great Depression of the 1930s caused millions of people throughout the United States to lose their jobs. Residents of Hershey were more fortunate. Instead of retreating, Milton Hershey charged forward. Although he had no way of knowing if sales of his chocolate products would

remain strong, Milton Hershey took advantage of a ready and able supply of labor and cheap raw materials to embark upon massive building and public works projects to benefit his community and its growing numbers of visitors and, in the process, to create over 600 jobs! It was another Hershey risk and even though sales of *Hershey's* chocolate were lower than in the 1920s, the corporation continued to turn a profit, and employment at the factory remained stable. Because of his

vision, Milton Hershey constructed numerous facilities designed to meet a wide range of recreational, cultural, and educational needs which still benefit the community of Hershey today. Possibly the most well known landmarks of this period are the Hershey Community Building and Theatre, completed in 1932, constructed in part to commemorate the upcoming 30th anniversary of the town; *The Hotel Hershey*, completed in 1933, whose architecture reflects the finest of Spanish Mediterranean traditions; the Junior–Senior High School of the Hershey Industrial School, completed in 1934, considered to be one of the finest art deco–designed buildings of its time; the Windowless Office Building of the Hershey Chocolate Corporation, completed in 1935, a building whose controlled environmental concept has since been copied hundreds of times the world over; and the *Hershey* Sports Arena, completed in 1936, the largest single span concrete structure in the world at the time of its completion. During this period of great economic hardship, Milton Hershey also saw to the spiritual well-being of his community by presenting each of the five churches in Hershey with a gift of $20,000. In 1935,

Canceled Trust Company Checks. The Trust Company and the Hershey Bank were both housed in the Trust Company building after charter of the bank in 1925. The building was expanded in 1967 with the addition of single-story wings to each side. The Trust Company moved its offices to High Point, Milton Hershey's former home, in 1991. Today, PNC Bank occupies the building.

he established the M.S. Hershey Foundation to provide for educational opportunities for residents of Derry Township and to specifically oversee operations of the Hershey Junior College established in 1938.

A PLACE TO VISIT

Milton Hershey capitalized on the public's interest in his town from its inception. He included postcards of Hershey, Pennsylvania, in his nickel chocolate bars. In 1915, a visitors bureau opened and chocolate factory tours were offered on an ongoing basis. By 1935, more than 50,000 people a year toured the factory. In 1916, the Hershey Zoo, the largest free private zoo in America at that time, was opened to the public. Until cars became the favored mode of transportation, trolleys provided cheap and easy access to Hershey. Milton Hershey continued to develop community facilities that would attract and entertain visitors. *Hershey Park* was one such facility which developed rapidly in response to visitor use and interest. The construction of numerous buildings and facilities in the 1930s, including the Hershey Community Center Building and Theatre, *The Hotel Hershey*, the *Hershey* Sports Arena and Stadium, the Hershey Rose Garden, and the Hershey Museum, transformed Hershey into a major tourist attraction, capable of entertaining thousands of people at a time. By the end of the 1930s, Hershey emerged as a nationally known tourist destination.

THE END OF AN ERA

Despite his increasing age and his voluntary removal from the day-to-day decision making of the town after 1927, Milton Hershey remained an active and beloved participant in the affairs of the community. On September 13, 1937, the community held a celebration in the recently completed Sports Arena honoring Milton Hershey's 80th birthday. Three

In 1913, the town celebrated its 10th anniversary in grand style. During those first years, Hershey grew from a small rural crossroads to a town complete with a consolidated school system, postal service, trolley service, a bank, a department store, rail service, phone service, and a volunteer fire company, as well as extensive recreational services, including a theater, a library, and a beautiful park.

Hershey Transit Company Trolley on Chocolate Avenue 1916. In 1903, Milton Hershey sponsored creation of a trolley system consisting of both freight and passenger service. Although the system extended into nearby towns and through miles of rural countryside, Chocolate Avenue (the main thoroughfare in Hershey) remained the hub of trolley activity. Here, milk trolleys from the surrounding dairy farms reached their unloading destination. Passengers bound for Sunday excursions to *Hershey Park*, to school, or to work usually passed through Chocolate Avenue. The "trolley barn" where trolleys were stored and serviced was also located along Chocolate Avenue. Like most small towns in America at this time, Hershey's main street was unpaved.

121

Trolley Tickets and Motormen Receipt Tags circa 1925.

years later, on his 83rd birthday, the American Rose Society named a rose in honor of Milton Hershey. After witnessing the end of World War II, the victory in Europe and the Japanese surrender, 88-year-old Milton Hershey passed away on October 13, 1945. Always interested in the welfare of the community that bears his name, Milton Hershey's personal estate at the time of his death was set aside and placed in a separate trust fund to ensure continued additional financial support for the Derry Township public school system. He was buried in the Hershey Cemetery in a family plot next to his wife, his mother, and his father. Although he left no heirs, Milton Hershey did leave behind a unique heritage and a securely established community and business. A new era of diversification, change, and growth was about to begin.

Manhole Covers 1922–1930. When establishing his town, Milton Hershey provided for all necessary public utilities. Prior to 1927, the Hershey Chocolate Company placed covers marked H.C.C. over sewer and water lines for the town. Those marked H. EST. were placed by Hershey Estates, which owned and maintained the town's municipal services beginning in 1928.

Convention Hall circa 1925. Dedicated on May 30, 1915, this building could seat up to 4,000 people for concerts, meetings, and group gatherings. Beginning in 1925, each December through April it was converted into the "Ice Palace" for skating and hockey. It was the original home to the American Hockey League's *Hershey Bears,* who now play in the neighboring *Hersheypark* Arena. In 1938, it was renovated and became home to the Hershey Museum.

High Point Mansion circa 1925. Built in the shadow of the Hershey Chocolate Factory, High Point served as the home of Mr. and Mrs. Hershey beginning in 1908. During its construction, the Hersheys lived in the Homestead. Compared with contemporary mansions built by such wealthy families as the Vanderbilts or Astors, the Hershey mansion was quite modest. The home originally contained 22 rooms and was built at a cost of $36,080.36. Total cost of the house, including furnishings, landscaping, and architectural services of C. Emlen Urban was approximately $100,000. Servants were limited to a housekeeper, houseman, and a housemaid. The Hersheys used professional decorators, but were also guided by their own tastes. Mrs. Hershey took great pleasure in designing and developing the gardens.

(Background) *Swan Lake, Hershey Mansion Grounds 1915.* Kitty Hershey took special pride in High Point's grounds, accenting them with potted palms and other trees. Swan Lake and several other artificial lakes were created by diverting water from Spring Creek, the small creek that ran between the factory and the mansion. The landscaping of the mansion's grounds was open to the public to enjoy. Located as close to the factory and the center of town as it was, the Hershey's home was very much a part of the community.

(Above) *Entertaining at High Point 1911.* Catherine Hershey (second from left) and Milton Hershey (fifth from left) are joined by unidentified guests on the porch of High Point. In this photo, Mr. Hershey is wearing golf shoes. Golf was a favorite pastime of his, which probably explains the existence of several quality courses in Hershey today.

(Below) *High Point Interior, Living Room circa 1910.* Mr. Hershey preferred an open design for the mansion's first floor. There were no doors between the living room, dining room, library, and entrance hall. The entry hall was specially designed to receive the cut glass torchère that Mr. Hershey purchased at the Colombian Exposition in 1893.

(Below) *High Point Interior, Dining Room circa 1910.* Mr. and Mrs. Hershey furnished their home with items purchased on their trips abroad or from shopping excursions to Philadelphia and New York. They relied heavily upon the services of The Chapman Decorative Company of Philadelphia for decorating

the mansion's interior. Although they could well afford the finest furniture, paintings, and home accessories, the Hershey's usually bought furnishings of good quality, but not necessarily the best or the most expensive.

(Background) *Homes along Cocoa Avenue, Looking South circa 1919.* The first homes for workers were built as early as 1907. Milton Hershey was not satisfied with the original homes since they were offered in only two styles. He wished to avoid the look of conformity present in most other company towns. The later variety of styles produced streetscapes similar to this throughout the town.

(Right) *The Torchère in the Entrance Hall of High Point Mansion circa 1938.* Today the torchère is the property of the Milton Hershey School and is on long-term loan to the Hershey Museum, where it has been on continuous display for many years.

(Below) *Entertaining on the Grounds of High Point 1911.* Relatively few photographs of Milton and Catherine Hershey survive from their years at High Point, which may be due in large part to Mrs. Hershey's illness. The arbor and pool in the background were one of Kitty Hershey's favorite places to spend time.

In this May 1937 photograph taken in the second-floor apartment study at High Point, Milton Hershey is 79 years old.

(Background) *The Hershey Department Store 1933.* The department store moved to the northwest corner of Chocolate Avenue and Park Drive to occupy the former Hershey Press Building in 1920. The department store discontinued operations on September 12, 1973. It has since served as home to numerous commercial enterprises.

(Above, left) *Homes along Chocolate Avenue, East End 1916.* The large homes in this area near High Point Mansion were primarily built for chocolate-company executives. In contrast to an average home of a worker which cost $2,000 to construct, these homes averaged more than $10,000.

(Above, right) *Homes along Chocolate Avenue, East End 1916.* As this photograph of executive homes taken from the factory roof illustrates, much of Hershey was laid out on open farmland. The shrubs in the lower left corner spell HERSHEY COCOA and were planted about 1910.

(Right) *Hershey Public School 1926.* In 1924, the M.S. Hershey Junior–Senior High School was built and donated to the community by Milton Hershey to handle the growing student population.

(Below) *Derry Township Public Schools 1933.*
In 1929, Milton Hershey also provided for the construction of a companion "state-of-the-art" Hershey Vocational School for the children of his town.

(Left) *Hershey Community Center Building 1933.* This structure was built on the site of the McKinley Building at the southeast corner of Chocolate and Cocoa Avenues. Completed in 1932, and dedicated one year later, it is six stories tall and covers nearly six acres of floor space. The design of the highly ornamented building was executed in the style of the Italian Renaissance. It contained several recreational areas, a hospital, and a world-class theater designed to host both films and live stage shows.

Interiors, Hershey Community Building 1933. The facility contained an indoor swimming pool, a gymnasium, a library, a game room, a cafeteria, and several social rooms. The Hershey Men's Club also moved from the Cocoa House to this facility, allowing the Hershey Women's Club (formerly the YWCA) to occupy the Cocoa House.

(Below) *Hershey Community Theatre 1933.* Opened to the public in 1933, the theatre retains all of its original Venetian-style grandeur and remains a premier showplace for feature films, theatrical productions, and other live entertainment in south central Pennsylvania. It is now operated as a division of the nonprofit M.S. Hershey Foundation as a cultural resource for the community of Hershey.

Hershey Community Center Building 1963–69. Throughout most of its existence, the Community Center remained the center for community recreation and entertainment. In 1963, WHRY-AM and WMSH-FM began broadcasting from the building. One year later, WITF Educational Television went on air with a studio located in the basement of the building. Between 1938 and 1965, the building also housed the Hershey Junior College. In 1981, the building was placed on the National Register of Historic Places. In 1982, most of the building (except for the Hershey Theatre) became home to Hershey Foods Corporation's Corporate Administrative Center.

Hershey American Indian Museum 1933. Milton Hershey created the museum in 1933 as yet another cultural resource for visitors and residents of the community. The museum was originally housed in a limestone building a short distance from the factory. It offered a premier collection of Native American objects and cultural material from throughout North America.

The Hershey Museum circa 1940. In 1935, Milton Hershey purchased a large collection of Pennsylvania German artifacts from Lancaster County. No longer able to house both collections in the original building, Hershey had the former Convention Hall renovated as a site for the museum. After three years of remodeling, the "New" Hershey Museum opened to the public on November 12, 1938, in its present location. The adjoining sports arena referred to in the promotional sign below opened in December 1936.

Garden Terrace

Dining Room

Patio and Main Lounge

East Portico

AN unusual hotel of quiet dignity, refinement and pleasant surroundings away from the noise and congestion of the city . . . a delightful place to sojourn for a few days or for a permanent residence. Open the year 'round.

Corner of Patio

Single Bedroom

Parlor of Suite

Double Bedroom

The Hotel Hershey *1933*. The design of *The Hotel Hershey*, opened to the public in 1933, was based on some of Milton Hershey's favorite Mediterranean hotels. Placed on a hill overlooking the town to the south and the Blue Mountains to the north, the 170-room hotel was designed to provide the latest in comfort and leisure activities for its guests.

Published as a guide for guests of the hotel, the first issue of *Hotel Hershey High-Lights* appeared on May 5, 1934, and its last on June 17, 1950. This issue is from 1939.

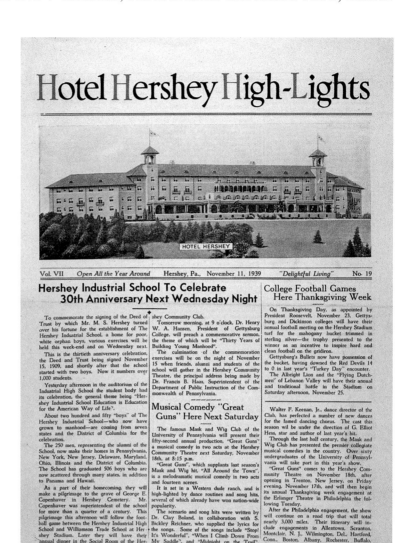

Postcard circa 1945. "Color immediately attracts the eye as one enters the Patio of *The Hotel Hershey*. The Patio suggests the outdoors, the illusion being created by slanting colored tile roofs, awnings, and a realistic sky painted overhead. The stone walks are harmoniously colored and the rugs give the appearance of closely cropped grass. In the center is a fountain, the falling water having a pleasing effect."

(Left) In addition to modernizing production facilities, Hershey pioneered office-building design with one of the nation's first windowless office buildings. Built on the site of the original three buildings of the Hershey Chocolate Company, this stunning example of art deco design, completed near the end of 1935, provided a controlled environment for the office staff. It featured central air conditioning, planned artificial lighting, glass partitions in place of walls, and seascapes and other outdoor scenes painted on walls in place of windows. Descriptions of the building at the time of its opening claimed it to be "Science's latest work to aid workers at Hershey." This post-card is from the mid-'40s.

(Right) In the spring of 1937, the Hershey Rose Garden, located adjacent to *The Hotel Hershey* on seven acres of sloped land, opened to the public. This 1940 postcard reads, "On days when the water is still, the pool of the Hershey Rose Garden reflects the various colors of the Roses of the World, and the attractive surroundings. The Hershey Rose Garden contains more than 30,000 rose

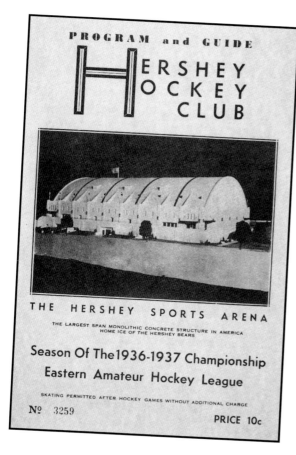

PROGRAM and GUIDE
HERSHEY HOCKEY CLUB

THE HERSHEY SPORTS ARENA

THE LARGEST SPAN MONOLITHIC CONCRETE STRUCTURE IN AMERICA
HOME ICE OF THE HERSHEY BEARS

**Season Of The 1936-1937 Championship
Eastern Amateur Hockey League**

SKATING PERMITTED AFTER HOCKEY GAMES WITHOUT ADDITIONAL CHARGE

Nº 3259   PRICE 10c

plants of over 700 distinct varieties, in bloom from June to frost time." Now under the auspices of the M.S. Hershey Foundation, the Hershey Gardens have developed into a 23-acre botanical garden featuring seasonal flowering displays, collections of specimen trees and shrubs, themed garden areas, and an award-winning rose garden.

(Opposite, bottom) *The **Hershey** Sports Arena circa 1938.* The arena first opened in December 1936 as home of the *Hershey Bears*, members of the Eastern Amateur Hockey League. The team actually began as the *Hershey B'ars*, but quickly changed their name to one sounding less commercial. In 1938, the team joined the American Hockey League. They remain a successful AHL franchise, having most recently won the Calder Cup (the league's championship trophy) in the 1996–97 season.

***Hershey** Sports Arena Postcard circa 1945.* "The colorful *Hershey* Sports Arena, largest span concrete monolithic structure in America. Home to the American Hockey League *Hershey Bears*, Ice-Skating Revues and public skating from mid-October through mid-March. Also used for professional, college, and high school basketball, professional wrestling and conventions. Can seat 7,200 for sporting events and 10,000 for conventions."

(Below) *As Hershey Looked from the Air in 1923.*

From bar cards in the 1910s through retail point-of-purchase displays, window advertising, and educational materials, Milton Hershey saw the value of tying the town and product of Hershey inexorably together. This is the back cover of the 1926 edition of "The Story of Chocolate and Cocoa."

It is only natural that some of the buildings in Hershey would eventually grace product packaging and product lines as well. Specialty chocolates such as the *Old Homestead* line actually featured postcards attached to box lids. Others, such as the *Hotel Hershey Sweets* line, harkened back to the boutique-style packaging and sense of exclusivity chocolate represented at the turn of the century.

Hershey Celebrates Its 50th Anniversary.

The Homestead—Hershey Industrial School circa 1913.

(Below) *Postcard of the Homestead Postmarked August 10, 1945.* "From this building is directed the activities of the almost 1,000 orphan boys Mr. Hershey is educating by heart, mind and hand to give them a start in life and become useful citizens in the communities where they expect to make their homes after they graduate from the Hershey Industrial School."

(Above) *Postcard of the Homestead circa 1920.* (Below) By April 1933, the school included 22 dormitories each housing between 14 and 28 boys.

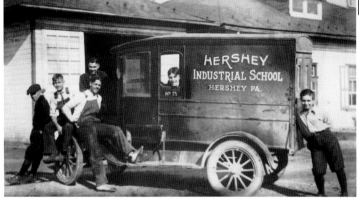

(Above) *"Homeboys" 1922–1923.*

(Above) *Milton S. Hershey with Student Boys at the Hershey Industrial School 1923.*

(Right) *Mr. Hershey, the Philanthropist.* Milton S. Hershey is pictured here in 1923 with Robert Coleman Sheaffer, who later graduated from the school.

Postcard of Junior–Senior High School Postmarked August 14, 1936. "Hershey Industrial Junior–Senior High School in foreground and *The Hotel Hershey* in background." Located just north of the town of Hershey, the building opened with a faculty of 35 and an enrollment of 352 students in grades 6 through 12. It is now known as Senior Hall and serves the Milton Hershey School as its high school.

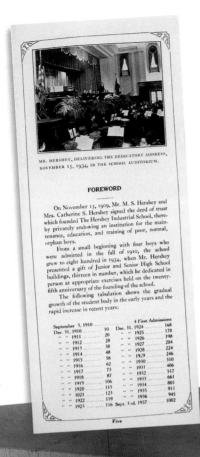

Taken from the Booklet "A Brief Description of The Hershey Industrial School" 1938.
(Left) Enrollment figures for the Hershey Industrial School.
(Right) Household Division.

MR. HERSHEY, DELIVERING THE DEDICATORY ADDRESS, NOVEMBER 15, 1934, IN THE SCHOOL AUDITORIUM.

FOREWORD

On November 15, 1909, Mr. M. S. Hershey and Mrs. Catherine S. Hershey signed the deed of trust which founded The Hershey Industrial School, thereby privately endowing an institution for the maintenance, education, and training of poor, normal, orphan boys.

From a small beginning with four boys who were admitted in the fall of 1910, the school grew to eight hundred in 1934, when Mr. Hershey presented a gift of Junior and Senior High School buildings, thirteen in number, which he dedicated in person at appropriate exercises held on the twenty-fifth anniversary of the founding of the school.

The following tabulation shows the gradual growth of the student body in the early years and the rapid increase in recent years:

September 3, 1910		4 First Admissions	
Dec. 31, 1910	10	Dec. 31, 1924	168
" " 1911	20	" " 1925	178
" " 1912	28	" " 1926	198
" " 1913	38	" " 1927	204
" " 1914	48	" " 1928	224
" " 1915	58	" " 1929	246
" " 1916	62	" " 1930	310
" " 1917	73	" " 1931	406
" " 1918	87	" " 1932	517
" " 1919	106	" " 1933	661
" " 1920	115	" " 1934	801
" " 1921	123	" " 1935	911
" " 1922	119	" " 1936	945
" " 1923	116	Sept. 3rd 1937	1002

Five

A TYPICAL HOME UNIT

THE HOUSEHOLD DIVISION

Boys are housed in home units. The junior boys live in groups of twenty to thirty, with a house-mother to each ten boys. On the farms, where the boys of sixth grade and above live, the average group number is twenty, and there the farmer has disciplinary authority. Each boy of whatever age has his own bed, with such locker, chest, and closet space as is necessary, and these the boys—except the very little ones—must care for and keep in order.

All have good wholesome food in plentiful variety. There is no routine of meals. A boy never knows what will be served at the next day's table. But a boy who is well must eat what is placed before him. If there is a dish he professes not to like, he must eat at least a small portion. A healthy child soon learns to like what he sees his mates eat, and nothing is ever offered a boy but what is proper to his years and health. Our own farms and extensive gardens garnish the tables abundantly.

THE CAFETERIA

HOME UNIT DINING ROOM

THE CENTRAL KITCHEN

HOME UNIT BED ROOM

Eight

Nine

The Hershey Industrial School Carpentry Shop in the 1910s.

Graduation at the Hershey Industrial School 1948.

Souvenir Football Program 1943. In 1943, Hershey Industrial School began a football rivalry with Hershey High School that continues to this day. The annual Cocoa Bean Game is sponsored each year by the Rotary Club of Hershey as a community fund-raiser.

In Memoriam circa 1945. Graduates of the Hershey Industrial School proudly served their country during World War II. A substantial number of these men also gave their lives in defense of their country.

Perhaps Milton Hershey's death on October 14, 1945, one month after his 88th birthday, affected the young men of the school the hardest. They were "his boys" and in a very literal sense, his only real family. To most of the boys, Milton Hershey was likewise part of their family. The November 1945 issue of the school magazine, *The School Industrialist*, printed and published by the Hershey Industrial School Press, was devoted exclusively to the life of Milton Hershey. The photograph of Mr. Hershey on the front cover was from a formal studio portrait taken in 1938.

(Above) *Milton Hershey School 1953*. In December 1951, the Industrial School was renamed the Milton Hershey School. This two-page spread on the school appeared in the town's 50th-anniversary publication.

*Children's Playground, **Hershey Park** 1915*. Picnicking was a favorite pastime in the park during its early years. Special excursion trains and trolleys brought large groups from surrounding communities. Visitors enjoyed the playground, baseball, band concerts, and canoeing on Spring Creek.

*Miniature Trolley and Merry-Go-Round, **Hershey Park** 1916.*

*Boating at **Hershey Park**. The postcard reads, "Picturesque vistas, blooming shrubs, flowers, well kept trees, and manicured lawns make Hershey Park a cool, delightful resort when summer reigns."*

*The Swimming Pool at **Hershey Park**. The park pool opened in July 1929. This photo postcard is from 1932.*

(Left) This postcard, postmarked April 24, 1933, reads, "The Swimming Pool with locker accommodations for 3,500 is one of the most popular water resorts in Central Pennsylvania. The two pools are fed with sterilized water through high pressure chlorinating filters, and kept at just the right temperature."

(Upper right corner) This postcard, postmarked April 20, 1933, reads, "This $75,000 Electric Fountain and the Sunken Garden are located at the west end of *Hershey Park*. The fountain is operated entirely automatically by Thyraton tube control. It is a 35-projector fountain which consists of five small fountains built into one basin with the colors and jets so coordinated that the same combination on any two of the fountains will not appear at the same time. Thirty minutes are required for one cycle of the colored lighting effects."

(Upper left) This postcard, circa 1929–1935, reads, "Hershey teaches its employees not only how to work but how to play. In *Hershey Park* there is every facility for indoor and outdoor sport. The *Hershey Park* pool, with its 50-foot water toboggan, will accommodate several thousand bathers."

(Above) This Park Golf Club postcard postmarked May 8, 1933, reads, "This magnificent stone clubhouse provides excellent accommodations for the patrons of the *Hershey Park* Public Golf Course, which is considered one of the sportiest 18-hole courses in the state."

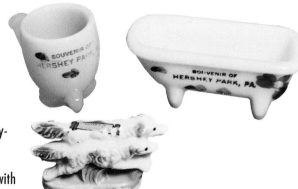

Hershey Park *Souvenirs circa 1930s.* As they do today, souvenirs provided a lasting momento of an enjoyable event. Many inexpensive souvenirs were mass-produced and simply stamped with the name of a venue, such as these milk glass pieces. Whenever possible, Hershey also took the opportunity to include scenes of "Beautiful *Hershey Park*" on souvenirs.

Chapter 6

Hershey Chocolate
"First in Favor and Flavor"

WE WANT T
WORKERS

HE HERSHEY
BACK TO WORK

On Hershey's main street, Chocolate Avenue, loyal workers and farmers paraded past the plant on April 7, 1937, in response to a sit-down strike which commenced on April 2.

THE CRASH OF '29

Two years after the National City Company had helped with the first issue launch of the Hershey Chocolate Corporation stock in 1927, Stanley Russell of National City approached Milton Hershey with a plan to form a large food conglomerate. In an age characterized by corporate mergers and acquisitions, Russell wished to consolidate Hershey with Colgate-Palmolive-Peet Corporation and the Kraft Phoenix Cheese Corporation to create an imposing food manufacturing and distribution system. In July 1929, Russell personally met with Milton Hershey and persuaded him to accept $100 per share for 500,000 shares of Hershey common stock—a $50 million transaction. His option was $1 a share, or $500,000. An initial payment of $250,000 by National City Company sealed the arrangement. Even in its planning stages, the proposed food merger was big news. The next few months saw Hershey's common stock climb to a high of 150 $^1/_2$. National City Company's risk looked sound. But few, if any, sensed that the stock market was poised at the edge of an abyss as the year 1929 headed into its final months. With the crash of the stock market on October 29, the day known as Black Tuesday, the prosperity of the 1920s came to a screeching halt. By November 14, Hershey common stock had plummeted to a dismal $45 per share. National City Company's plan disintegrated. However, as required, it did manage to pay Hershey the remaining half of his option. In the supposed win–win situation promised from the start, only Milton Hershey came out on top.

Mr. Goodbar circa 1935. During the 1920s, Hershey introduced two highly successful items that proved to be extremely popular with consumers and are still manufactured today. *Mr. Goodbar*, the first product, was introduced in 1925. The original advertising label promoted the confection as "chuck full of peanuts." *Hershey's* syrup was the other major success.

Hershey's Cocoa/Chocolate Syrup Displays circa 1930s.

Recipe Booklet 1948. This folded eight-page booklet was designed to fit into any "regular size" home-cooking index file. The recipe categories included Candies and Sauces, Cakes and Frostings, Desserts, Beverages, and Cookies.

Salesman's Sample Kit 1934–1937. This collapsible folder contains "dummy bar" samples from the standard *Hershey's* chocolate bar line during these years. A number of these bars were produced for only a short period, including the *Honey-Almond* milk chocolate bar (1926–1942), *Mild and Mellow* (1933–1941), and *Not-So-Sweet* (1934–1937).

Nougat-Almond 1939. An unsuccessful product introduced during the waning years of the 1930s, this bar quickly disappeared from the marketplace.

Introduced in 1937, the *Aero* bar was made by aerating chocolate with the use of a vacuum to create a honeycomb-like texture. *Aero* had been a great success in England and Hershey licensed rights to manufacture this distinctly different type of chocolate from the Rowntree Chocolate Company Ltd. of England. The bar was popular, but the manufacturing process was very labor-intensive. Hershey stopped producing *Aero* in 1939.

THE STRIKE

The efforts of the federal government to stimulate industry and business during the Great Depression were not always successful. Many communities experienced violent labor unrest brought about by the failing economy. In late 1936, the recently formed CIO began a 44-day sit-down strike in a General Motors plant in Flint, Michigan. In a sit-down strike, employees stop working, but continue to occupy their workplace. The strike quickly spread to other industries, eventually involving millions of workers. Although largely shrouded from these violent upheavals, the Hershey Chocolate Corporation was not immune to pressures present in the rest of the nation. On April 2, 1937, a group of 400 to 600 workers, discontent over recent raise increases and with the support of the CIO, declared a sit-down strike at Hershey, shutting down chocolate production and barricading themselves in the plant. Town residents, nonstriking workers, and local dairy farmers (whose milk had no place to go) quickly responded by organizing parades and rallies in support of the company. On April 6, the strike was broken when loyal workers and farmers armed with clubs, baseball bats, pipes, and other weapons stormed the plant. On April 12, the Hershey Chocolate Corporation signed agreements with both the United Chocolate Workers of America,

affiliated with the CIO, and the Independent Chocolate Workers of Hershey, affiliated with the company loyalists, granting neither union exclusive bargaining rights, but protecting each from discrimination. Following a series of even more violent strikes in the coming months, the Supreme Court declared sit-down strikes to be illegal seizures of property in *National Labor Relations Board* v. *Fansteel Metallurgical Corporation* in 1939.

THE WAR EFFORT

As the dark clouds of the Depression gradually gave way to the dark clouds of international war, the Hershey Chocolate Corporation continued to work tirelessly for the good of the American people. In 1937, at the request of the U.S. Army and with Milton Hershey's unqualified support, Samuel Hinkle, then Hershey's Chief Chemist, began to work with Paul Logan of the U.S. Army Quartermasters' Department and a staff of chemists to develop a resistible high-energy chocolate ration bar that would sustain a soldier when he had nothing else to eat. Remembering the all-too-good-tasting chocolate bar of World War I, the army wished the bar to be nourishing, but not tasty. Hershey came up with a four-ounce bar known as the *Field Ration D*, made of chocolate, sugar, powdered skim

Biscrisp, a chocolate-covered biscuit, lasted only from November 1938 to September 1939. The *Biscrisp* formula was similar to that of today's *Kit Kat* crisp-wafer-in-chocolate bar, first distributed by Hershey under license from Rowntree MacKintosh of England in 1970.

Honey-Almond Bar circa 1930. This product was first introduced in 1926 as the *Honey-Almond* bar. Hershey marketed this bar under three different names before discontinuing it in 1941.

Choclatier *Tin 1930–1941.* Forerunner of *Hershey's* cocoa mix, *Hershey's Choclatier* was used as an additive for hot chocolate as well as to flavor ice cream. As a bulk container product, it was primarily sold only to soda fountains and restaurants for preparing beverages and desserts.

Chocolate Soldier *1935.* Vernon Grant, a noted commercial illustrator, created this point-of-purchase advertisement specifically for Hershey. The Chocolate Soldier advertised *Choclatier.*

Cocoa Coatings *1930s.* Both cocoa and chocolate were important aspects of the coatings business for Hershey during this period. Outside manufacturers purchased bulk amounts of cocoa for flavoring both chocolate- and nonchocolate-based products. These are two examples of commercial-grade cocoas manufactured by Hershey for wholesale and commercial customers. Note the prominent use of the "Baby-in-the-Bean" logo on the label.

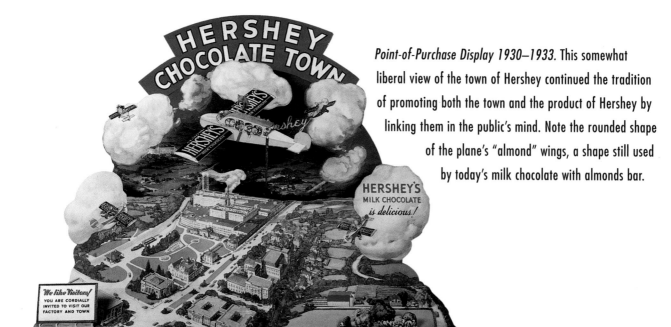

Point-of-Purchase Display 1930–1933. This somewhat liberal view of the town of Hershey continued the tradition of promoting both the town and the product of Hershey by linking them in the public's mind. Note the rounded shape of the plane's "almond" wings, a shape still used by today's milk chocolate with almonds bar.

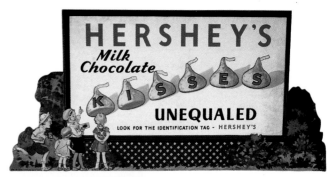

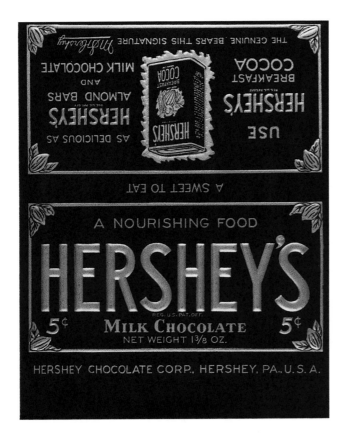

Milk Chocolate Label circa 1933–1935. Hershey used embossed labels like this until 1951. In the days before nutritional labels and UPC codes, the backs of bar wrappers were commonly used to advertise other company products.

Almond Milk Chocolate Display circa 1930s.

"A Kiss for You" Product Packaging 1928–1935. The late 1920s and early 1930s represented a period of transition in Milton Hershey's company and in the country at large, changes reflected even in the appearance of product

packaging. "A Kiss for You" boxes used to market *Hershey's Kisses* chocolates first appeared in the mid-1920s; the image was used on products for many years. The little white box in the upper left-hand corner of the image below first appeared about 1928 when the company became the Hershey Chocolate Corporation. Each of the boxes in this picture were produced after 1928 by the Corporation and, at first glance, seem very much the same. However, several different images appeared on the boxes during this period. Originally, the item count and size information appeared; soon after, an endorsement from the American Dental Association Committee on Foods was printed. From 1933 through 1935, Hershey proudly displayed the National Recovery Administration (NRA) Blue Eagle on the box. Following the dissolution of the NRA in 1935, the box quickly disappeared.

These "Good Because It's Hershey's" almond milk chocolate boxes also seem to be quite similar at first glance. They are all marked as products of the Hershey Chocolate Corporation, manufactured after 1927. However, the boxes on the left and in the center show an aerial view of the factory as it appeared before construction of the Windowless Office Building in December 1935. Hershey produced the first box between 1928 and 1932. The National Recovery Administration (NRA) image appeared on *Hershey's* product packages from 1933 through 1935. The box on the right shows the new addition to the factory (as well as an increase in traffic in more modern cars along Chocolate Avenue) and was produced beginning in 1936.

"The House of Hershey, Where Quality Is Paramount" appeared on a variety of product packages between 1920 and 1927. The green box on the left is for *Sweet Milk Chocolate* cakes while the center and right-hand boxes are for *Kisses Sweet Milk Chocolate*. The

two boxes on the left and center show a view of the factory taken from a promotional watercolor of the town and used on packaging and window displays since the 1910s. The box on the right shows the back of the factory along Chocolate Avenue with the HERSHEY COCOA bushes in the foreground.

Hershey's Bon-Bons 1930–1970. Not until the institution of a national advertising campaign in 1970 did Hershey begin to move away from packaging and promotions linking the town and product of Hershey. During these years, the traditional silver and maroon labeling still used today was often juxtaposed with packaging printed with various scenes and buildings around the town. The colorful box on the right dates from the late 1930s (the Windowless Office Building is on the bottom) and the brown and white box in the center is from the late 1960s.

milk, cocoa butter, vanillin, oats, and Vitamin B1. At 600 calories, it provided a subsistence diet. Perhaps because of the oats, it also met its taste requirement. Those forced to eat the *Field Ration D* bar have likened its taste to that of a boiled potato! The success of the *Field Ration D* bar was quickly followed by another Hershey-produced war ration, the *Tropical* chocolate bar. This chocolate bar was designed to withstand melting at high temperatures. All told, 1.6 billion ration bars were eventually shipped to Allied troops during World War II. As a result, the Hershey Chocolate Corporation was one of the few companies to be recognized five times with the Army–Navy "E" Production Award for high achievement.

NEW MANAGEMENT

Milton Hershey lived to see the end of World War II. He passed away on October 13, 1945, leaving behind both a unique heritage and a securely established business. The Hershey legacy was left in the hands of a man handpicked by Milton Hershey, the man who had directed his Cuban operations for many years: Percy Alexander Staples. While Milton Hershey was generally regarded as a risk taker and innovator, P. A. Staples was by nature a much more conservative man. He firmly believed that his one overriding responsibility lay in ensuring the perpetuation of the special Trust set up by Milton Hershey for the Industrial School. In order to strengthen the financial position of the company, he oversaw the sale of the Hershey properties in Cuba to the Cuban-Atlantic Sugar Company in 1946. At the time of the sale, Hershey's Cuban operations involved 65,000 acres of land and employed over 4,000 people in eight sugar mills and auxiliary services. During Staples' tenure, which ended with his death on July 23, 1956, Hershey manufactured only one new product of note: *Hershey-ets*, a candy-coated, disc-shaped chocolate confection, first manufactured in June 1954. Although they generally were years of stagnation for the company, the period did witness the restructuring of management and the recruitment of talented young people for positions as junior executives during Staples' tenure. Both of these changes were to have a long-term positive impact on the company and were primarily initiated by Samuel Hinkle in his role as plant manager, William Schiller as treasurer, Les Majer as secretary, and Jack Gallagher as sales manager—all four of whom moved forward despite the opposition of P.A. Staples. Staples' conservative nature and approach to business led to speculation that his concern about the vulnerability of the business to fluctuating commodities costs would someday lead him to sell the company. The board of directors quickly realized that investing so much power in the hands of one man was unwise.

A CHANGING OF THE GUARD

With the death of Staples in 1956, no one person would ever again hold all the top positions in the various industries and philanthropies of Hershey. And, for the first time, the Board was faced with setting in place a management structure not controlled or determined by Milton Hershey himself. Yet, despite the company's departure from a management style based upon the dominance of a single individual to one characterized by team leadership and cooperation, Milton Hershey remained the single most important inspiration for the company he had founded, built, and nurtured. His insistence upon honesty, integrity, and quality—both in the products he made and the people he employed—continue to be felt at all levels of the organization.

A MODERN CORPORATION

In the years after 1956, the young executives quickly rose to the top and began to make their mark in moving the company forward. Under the leadership of Samuel Hinkle, president of the Hershey Chocolate Corporation from 1956 until 1965, and Harold Mohler, his successor and president until 1976, a new breed of young, vigorous, expansion-minded

Hershey's Syrup Point-of-Purchase *Display 1934.*

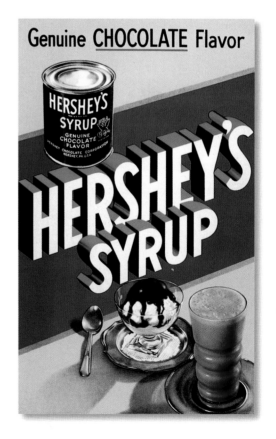

Genuine CHOCOLATE Flavor

HERSHEY'S SYRUP

Loyalty Parades 1937. The Hershey sit-down strike began on April 2, 1937. It ended five days later on April 7 when the strikers were forcibly removed from the factory by a coalition of loyal workers and local farmers whose milk could not get to the factory. The strike was a devastating blow to Milton Hershey, who suffered a stroke later that same year— the day after his 80th birthday.

Military Ration Bars 1937–1990. Hershey first developed the *Field Ration D* bar for the U.S. Army in September 1937. Over 1.6 billion ration bars were shipped to troops during World War II. During the war, the ingredient-mixing units in the discontinued *Kisses* molding department were utilized for tempering military ration bar chocolate paste. *Tropical* chocolate, a chocolate bar formulated to withstand melting at higher temperatures, was introduced in May 1943. After the war, *Tropical* chocolate bars became a standard component in many Coast Guard—approved emergency ration kits for both commercial and pleasure boats. On July 26, 1971, *Tropical* chocolate was sent to the moon with the astronauts of *Apollo 15.* In December 1990, Hershey delivered 144,000 similar heat-resistant *Desert Bars* to the Army for use in Operation Desert Storm in the Persian Gulf.

"Supplying Our Armed Forces" circa 1944. During World War II, much of *Hershey's* chocolate production was earmarked for the war effort. While it was difficult to find *Hershey's* products on the home front during these years, American soldiers were able to enjoy a sweet treat.

Hershey's Breakfast Cocoa 1942–1946. During World War II, Hershey modified its product line and packaging to aid in the effort to save metal. For instance, the aluminum can was replaced by a cardboard box with a metal lid. The cardboard was stained with iodine to achieve the look of the prewar label. Many consumers protested that the iodine affected the appearance and quality of the cocoa, and securing cans after the war was a top priority of the company.

Hershey's Mint Chocolate 1959. During the '50s and '60s, Hershey Chocolate experimented with a number of different kinds of candy-coated chocolates, including mint chocolate and *Hershey-ets*, as well as candy-coated peanuts and almonds. *Hershey's* mint chocolate was first introduced on February 2, 1959, and was discontinued in February 1969.

Hershey's Syrup Point-of-Purchase Display—"It's Great" 1930–1935. Hershey's syrup was an early form of convenience food when first introduced. Before then, homemakers had to make their own by boiling a concoction of cocoa, sugar, and water.

leaders emerged. They quickly saw the need for a greater manufacturing capacity and a more diversified product line. This led to the opening in 1963 of the Smith Falls, Ontario, plant in Canada—the first new manufacturing facility to be built outside of Hershey. In 1965, Hershey subsequently opened a West Coast chocolate and confectionery plant in Oakdale, California. It was also at this time that Hershey recognized the need for more professional marketing and sales talent. It had become clear that the company was losing market share and was unable to market new products successfully. Hershey's competitors had grown nicely, achieving a larger share of the market at Hershey's expense. It had become obvious that the company needed to generate more pull for its products through advertising. The first efforts at coordinated advertising were made in Canada in 1964 when Hershey Chocolate of Canada, Ltd. initiated a national advertising program, utilizing television and billboards throughout Canada.

ACQUISITION AND GROWTH

The expansion of Hershey under the presidency of Samuel Hinkle was a marked contrast to that of P. A. Staples. Hinkle's innovative style and willingness to take risks was reminiscent of Milton Hershey's own ways of doing things and like the company founder, the risks quickly paid off. Unlike Staples, Hinkle encouraged the introduction of several new and innovative products into the Hershey lineup. Some of the more noteworthy examples include *Hershey's* instant cocoa mix, introduced in September 1956; *Hershey's* mint chocolate, introduced in February 1959, and discontinued in February 1969; *Hershey's* vitamin-fortified syrup, introduced in September 1959, and discontinued in July 1963; *Hershey's* chocolate-covered candy-coated almonds, introduced in October 1959, and discontinued in 1972; *Hershey's* sweet milk cocoa, introduced in February 1962; *Hershey's* Pennsylvania

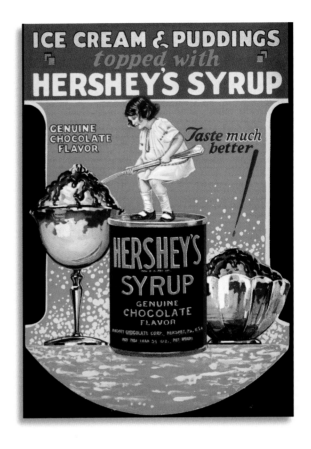

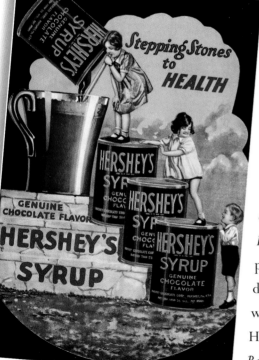

Dutch sweet chocolate, introduced in November 1962, and discontinued in 1968; *Hershey's* butter chip bar, introduced in February 1963, and discontinued in September 1968; *Hershey's Handi-Bake*, a liquid baking product, introduced in November 1964, and discontinued in February 1969; and *Hershey's* chocolate-covered candy-coated peanuts, introduced in March 1965, and discontinued in December 1978. Hinkle was also instrumental in acquiring the H.B. Reese Candy Co., Inc., makers of *Reese's* peanut butter cups, in 1963, and overseeing the expansion of the Corporation into Canada and California. With Harold Mohler as president in 1966, Hershey embarked upon new ventures into pasta manufacturing with

Syrup was produced by heating a mixture of cocoa powder, sugar, water, and flavoring. It was made in several different varieties. The most common variety was used in the home to put on ice cream, mix with hot or cold milk, or to make puddings and icing for cake. The remaining types were sold in bulk for commercial use as flavoring agents in soda fountains and ice cream. Hershey was the first to sell chocolate syrup for home use. These images are from the early to mid-'30s.

Hershey's Cocoa circa 1925.
The familiar block letters spelling
HERSHEY'S COCOA first appeared in
1924 on cocoa tin labels. Until 1936,
cocoa labels incorporated the
"Baby-in-the-Bean" trademark.

the acquisition of the San Giorgio Macaroni, Inc. and Delmonico Foods, Inc. companies. Under Mohler, Hershey Chocolate Corporation of Canada, Ltd. continued to expand as well by acquiring David & Frere, Ltd. of Montreal, Quebec, in 1967. Recognizing its growth in both chocolate and nonchocolate operations as well as its diversification into the pasta market, the company reorganized for the first time since it had gone public in 1927. On February 19, 1968, the Hershey Chocolate Corporation changed its name to Hershey Foods Corporation and adopted a new corporate logo to replace the "Baby-in-the-Bean" trademark which had been in use since 1898. The new corporation consisted of two operating divisions: chocolate and related manufacturing was placed with the Hershey Chocolate and Confectionery Division and pasta manufacturing with the Hershey Pasta Division.

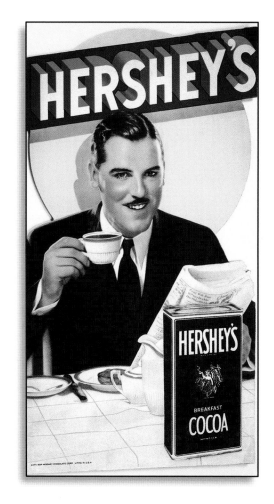

(Above, left) *Hershey's* Breakfast Cocoa 1934. This lithographed point-of-purchase retail display was used to promote a steaming cup of hot cocoa as the perfect breakfast beverage. The word BREAKFAST above cocoa first appeared on cocoa tins in 1928.

(Above) *Hershey's* Cocoa Display 1937.

(Left) *Hershey's* Cocoa Display 1930–1935. In a window or promotional display, the cutout was designed to hold an actual 5 1/2-ounce can of *Hershey's* syrup.

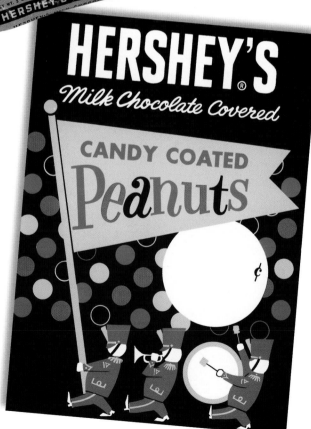

Hershey-ets *1954. Hershey-ets* were first introduced on June 24, 1954. These popular candies were made by bonding two chocolate chips together and covering them with a thin sugar shell. The distinctive football shape set them apart from the competing candy-coated chocolates. They were discontinued in November 1978. But beginning in 1983, Hershey reintroduced packages of red and green *Hershey-ets* for the Christmas season. *Hershey-ets* have become a popular seasonal confection at Christmas and are now available in several other seasonal colors as well.

Hershey introduced Milk Chocolate Covered Candy Coated Peanuts on March 23, 1965. Although they tasted good, they could not successfully compete with a similar, already well established competitor's product. They were discontinued in December 1978.

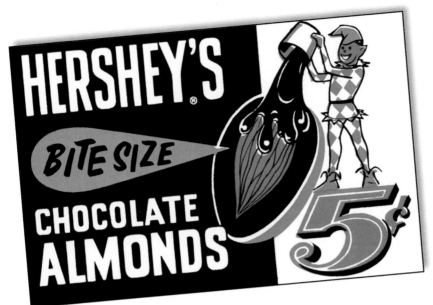

Hoping to build upon the popularity of *Hershey's* milk chocolate bar with almonds, the company introduced milk chocolate–covered candy-coated almonds in October 1959. This product was discontinued in 1972, but a similar product, *Golden Almond Solitaires*, was much more successful when introduced in 1984.

Krackel *Chocolate Bar Display 1956.* One of Hershey Chocolate's most enduring confectionery products is their *Krackel* chocolate bar introduced on September 14, 1938. However, the original formula changed a number of times during its first years. At first, *Krackel* also included almonds, and later peanuts, as well as crisped rice in its formula. The nuts were eliminated in 1943. Since then the recipe for *Krackel* has changed very little.

Hershey's Krackel Promotional Offer 1965.

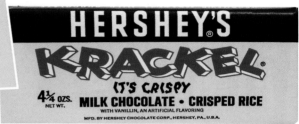

Hershey's Krackel 1962.

Bitter-Sweet Chocolate 1937–1944.

Semi-Sweet Chocolate 1949–1955. The first Hershey's sweet chocolate products were manufactured in Lancaster in 1894. With the introduction of milk chocolate in 1900, sweet chocolate became a less important product line. In January 1934, Hershey reentered the sweet chocolate market in a big way with the Not-So-Sweet chocolate bar. It remained in production until November 1937 when it was replaced with the Bitter-Sweet chocolate bar. Hershey discontinued the manufacture of Bitter-Sweet in February 1944. In 1949, Hershey again reintroduced a sweet chocolate product, this time with a less harsh sounding name. The Semi-Sweet bar was in turn replaced with the Special Dark bar, described as mildly sweet chocolate, in October 1971.

On June 9, 1941, Hershey Chocolate introduced its "First in Favor and Flavor" slogan for use on its candy bars. It was used on chocolate bar advertisements and on the back of the bars themselves until the mid-1960s.

Milk Chocolate Bar 1950–1955.

Between 1958 and 1964, the "First in Favor and Flavor" slogan was also used on shipping boxes.

Advertising on Trucks circa 1965. Advertising can take all kinds of forms. At one time, Hershey maintained its own fleet of milk delivery trucks, which were also used to advertise various products. These particular trucks, parked at the East End of the chocolate factory where the garages were located, reflect the diversity of the *Hershey's* product line. Like bar cards, box and bar labels, and point-of-purchase counter and window displays, these trucks represent an innovative and economical approach to effective advertising.

Advertising on Trucks circa 1968. Even though Hershey no longer maintains its own fleet of milk trucks, trucks continue to be an important resource for moving raw materials and finished product. The cabs of these trucks sport the Hershey Foods name and logo adopted by the company in 1968.

Soft Packaging, Commercial Sale circa 1950s.

Seasonal Promotion, Retail Sales Flyer, Halloween 1956.

Seasonal Promotion, Retail Sales Flyer, Christmas circa 1955–1960.

(Below) **Hershey's** Instant Cocoa Mix 1956–1968. Hershey's instant cocoa mix debuted in September 1956. In 1968, Hershey Chocolate stopped domestic production of this product and instead used its Canadian plant (opened in 1963) to manufacture instant cocoa mix. The tin pictured on the right was manufactured in Canada circa 1968 for domestic use and is indicative of the historic economic interdependence and growing interrelationship between the two North American trading partners.

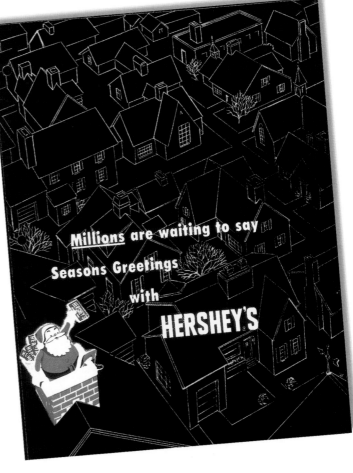

(Right) Reverse, Instant Cocoa Mix Tin circa 1956.

(Above) *Vitamin Fortified Syrup, Produced between September 1959 and July 1963.*

Hershey's *Butter Chip, Produced between February 1963 and September 1968.*

Hershey's Handi-Bake, *Produced between November 1964 and February 1969.*

Hershey's *Pennsylvania Dutch Sweet Chocolate, Produced between February 1962 and September 1968.*

H.B. Reese Candy Company 1923–1963. H.B. Reese began making confectionery products in the basement of his own home at 18 East Areba Avenue in Hershey in 1923. From 1923 until 1928, he made a variety of marginally successful confectionery products. In 1926, he moved to a new factory at 205 West Caracas Avenue and began coating an assortment of candy with chocolate purchased from Hershey Chocolate Co. A new item, a chocolate-covered peanut butter cup, was added to the assortment in 1928. Conditions during World War II prompted H.B. Reese to discontinue his other candy lines and concentrate on the "penny cup." That decision developed into something truly unique in America's food industry—a major company built and thriving on one product alone, the *Reese's* peanut butter cup. The H.B. Reese Candy Company enjoyed a long and friendly relationship with Hershey Chocolate before its acquisition by Hershey in 1963. With this acquisition, Hershey gained a quality confectionery company and its popular product.

The present Reese's plant on the west edge of the town of Hershey was first put into operation on August 1, 1957. It has been expanded several times and now occupies several hundred thousand square feet. Since its acquisition by Hershey in 1963, the *Reese's* product line has expanded to include the *Kit Kat* bar, *Reese's* peanut butter, *Reese's Pieces* candies, the *Nutrageous* bar, and *ReeseSticks*.

Cupping Department, Reese Candy Company 1936. H.B. Reese first produced his now-famous peanut butter cup in 1928. This photograph shows women preparing trays with paper cups, which were then filled with a layer of chocolate, the peanut butter center, and then with more chocolate.

"For a Christmas Not Only Merry But Big" circa 1963–1965. Soon after the acquisition of H.B. Reese Candy by Hershey, promotional advertising quickly and effectively emphasized the new relationship between *Reese's* and *Hershey's.*

Halloween Promotion 1967.

Chapter 7

New taste treat!

New HERSHEY-E

HERSHEY'S MILK

HERSHEY'S MILK CHOCO

HERSHEY'S MILK CHOCO

The Great American
Chocolate Company

The popular *Hershey-ets* with their distinctive football shape were produced from June 1954 until November 1978.

A NATIONAL ADVERTISING CAMPAIGN

The same year that Hershey Chocolate Corporation changed its name to Hershey Foods Corporation to reflect its increasingly diversified business, Hershey announced its plan to initiate a national consumer advertising campaign and entered into an agreement with Ogilvy & Mather to become the corporation's advertising agency. On July 19, 1970, Hershey Foods inaugurated its campaign with a Sunday newspaper supplement advertisement. On September 19, 1970, Hershey instituted a companion television and radio advertising program as well. It did not take long for Hershey to realize the benefits of advertising. While sales for the milk chocolate bar and the milk chocolate with almond bar did not rise dramatically at the time, sales of *Reese's* peanut butter cups and *Hershey's Kisses* chocolates grew significantly. In today's highly competitive chocolate and confectionery business, advertising in magazines, television, radio, and other mass-market media is critical to the success of standard as well as new products. However, true to the tenets of Milton Hershey, a fresh, high-quality product has been and remains the best form of advertisement. Today, it's impossible to overstate the value of the *Hershey's* name and what it stands for in the consumer's mind in terms of quality, value, and taste.

Reese's Pieces candies are bite-sized pieces of peanut butter penuche covered with a candy shell. They were first introduced on September 7, 1978. Sales of the candy were given a tremendous boost when they were featured in *E.T.*, the 1982 movie about a winsome extraterrestrial. This was the biggest single promotion ever undertaken by Hershey for a single brand to that date.

GROWTH AND DIVERSIFICATION

Since the implementation of a national advertising campaign in 1970 and under the guiding hands of Harold Mohler and William Dearden in the 1970s and early 1980s, Hershey Foods Corporation continued to grow and diversify as part of its effort to become a major consumer food products company specializing in chocolate, confectionery, chocolate-related grocery, and dry pasta products. In 1970, Hershey acquired the rights from the English candy company Rowntree MacKintosh to manufacture and market *Rolo* caramels in milk chocolate, *Kit Kat* wafer bars, and *After Eight* chocolate dinner mints. In 1971, Hershey began production of *Hershey's Special Dark* candy bar (itself a reformulation of *Hershey's* semi-sweet candy bar). In 1977, Hershey introduced *Hershey's Golden Almond* chocolate bar, which prior to this had been available locally as the *50–50* bar. Under Dearden, Hershey widened its leading position in the confectionery market with the purchase of Y&S Candies, manufacturers of *Twizzlers* licorice and other licorice-type products, on November 30, 1977. However, the Corporation never lost sight of its core manufacturing priority and the strength of the *Hershey's* name. On August 7, 1978, the Chocolate and Confectionery Division of Hershey Foods was renamed Hershey Chocolate Company. Only one month later, Hershey introduced *Reese's Pieces* candies and the *Whatchamacallit* candy bar. As part of its ongoing effort to expand its share of the pasta business, Hershey acquired the Procino-Rossi Corporation's pasta-making operation in 1978 and the Skinner Macaroni Company in 1979. On November 6, 1979, Hershey Foods Corporation achieved $1 billion in annual sales for the first time and on December 31, 1981, only two short years

later, the Hershey Chocolate Company, the largest division of Hershey Foods, achieved $1 billion in annual sales for the first time. This amazing growth soon led the Hershey Chocolate Company to open a fourth manufacturing facility in Stuarts Draft, Virginia, on October 5, 1982, to join those already in operation in Pennsylvania, Canada, and California. In 1983, Hershey introduced *Hershey's* chocolate milk, its first premixed chocolate drink, and a number of confectionery items, including *Reese's Pieces* candies and the *Golden Pecan* and *Take Five* candy bars. On November 16, 1984,

*Christmas **Miniatures** Trade Advertisement 1970. Hershey's Miniatures chocolate bars were introduced in 1939 after years of using miniature sample bars to promote new products. Originally, Miniatures consisted of Milk Chocolate, Bitter-Sweet, Aero, Nougat-Almond, and Krackel bars.*

(Left) In 1990, the company first ventured into aseptic packaging—that is, packaging not requiring refrigeration.

(Below) In honor of the 100th anniversary in 1994, Hershey issued a series of several commemorative chocolate bars reminiscent of these produced between 1915 and 1920.

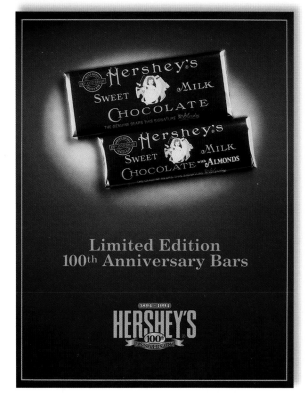

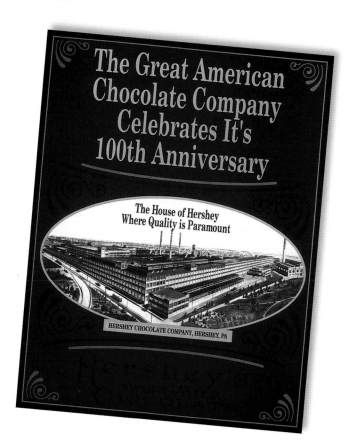

Kit Kat is the mainstay of Rowntree MacKintosh products, part of the Hershey family since 1970.

The look of *Mr. Goodbar* product packaging and wrapping has changed over the years, but the basic ingredients and quality have not. *Mr. Goodbar* has been a mainstay of the Hershey product family since November 20, 1925. (Below) Circa 1930s–1950s. (Left) Circa 1987.

Whatchamacallit 1988. This candy
bar was introduced in December 1978.

Hershey Foods Corporation also acquired the American Beauty Macaroni Company and added it to its pasta-manufacturing division.

ANOTHER GENERATION TAKES OVER

With the retirement of William Dearden in 1985, the mantle of leadership passed to yet another generation of progressive, innovative, and expansion-minded managers led by Richard Zimmerman and Kenneth Wolfe. In 1986, Hershey introduced *Hershey's Grand Slam* and *BarNone* candy bars and announced the purchase of the confectionery operations of the Dietrich Corporation, manufacturers of various chocolate and nonchocolate products including the *5th Avenue* candy bar and *Luden's* throat drops. On December 8, 1986, the Corporation announced that it had reached $2 billion in annual sales for the first time. In June 1987, Hershey Canada, Inc. acquired the assets of the Canadian confectionery and snack nut businesses of Nabisco Brands Ltd., and Hershey Chocolate introduced *Hershey's Golden Almond Nuggets* candy. Recognizing the growth of international sales as a significant proportion of corporate-wide sales and earnings, Hershey Foods Corporation once again reorganized to allow each new division to refocus its strategy on a particular market. On January 4, 1988, the Hershey Chocolate Company, the largest operating division of Hershey Foods Corporation, was officially renamed Hershey Chocolate U.S.A., allowing it to concentrate on the domestic chocolate market. Chocolate and nonchocolate confections manufactured under various domestic manufacturing and licensing agreements or as a result of their outright acquisition by Hershey could also be manufactured under their own product name or that of Hershey Foods Corporation.

ADDING VALUE—AN ONGOING COMMITMENT TO EXCELLENCE

As part of its ongoing effort to improve its position in the domestic marketplace, on August 25, 1988, Hershey Foods Corporation acquired the operating assets of Peter Paul/Cadbury's North American confectionery operations. Hershey Foods purchased the rights to manufacture, market, and distribute Peter Paul/Cadbury's U.S. confectionery brands including *Peter Paul Mounds*, *Peter Paul Almond Joy*, *York* peppermint pattie, and *Caramello*, among other products. On February 12, 1990, Hershey Foods announced the purchase of Ronzoni Foods Corporation from Kraft General Foods. The operating assets of the company, a manufacturing facility in Long Island City, New York, and a variety of dry pastas, pasta sauces, and cheese products became part of the Hershey Pasta Group, a name adopted by the Hershey Pasta Division in 1984. In February 1993, the Hershey Pasta Group opened a new state-of-the-art manufacturing plant in Winchester, Virginia. The opening of the Winchester plant coincided with the opening of yet another chocolate-manufacturing plant for Hershey Chocolate U.S.A. This brand-new state-of-the-art chocolate-manufacturing facility is located in Hershey and is known as West Hershey because of its relative location to the main Hershey plant. West Hershey joins the H.B. Reese Candy Company plant and the main Hershey plant as the only Hershey Foods manufacturing facilities located in the town of Hershey. In March of that same year, the Hershey Pasta Group acquired the operating assets and trademarks of the Ideal Macaroni Company, the Mrs. Weiss Noodle Company, and Pranzo D'Oro Inc., making it the leading U.S. manufacturer of dry pasta products under a

Skor 1985. Introduced in February 1981, *Skor* was originally licensed to Hershey from A.B. Marabou, Sweden, a leading Scandinavian confection company.

Hershey's Special Dark *1978.* Hershey introduced *Special Dark* on October 18, 1971. Despite undergoing a number of packaging changes and a formula reformulation, it remains another popular member of the Hershey family of fine products. The *Special Dark Big Block* was introduced in January 1980.

Hershey's *Milk Chocolate with Crisped Rice 1989.* The company launched a short-lived effort to increase product awareness through the use of Hershey's maroon and silver label. Despite market research to the contrary, the new label failed to catch on with consumers.

Luden's, Inc. circa 1940. William H. Luden founded the company that bears his name in Reading, Pennsylvania, in 1879. The Luden Corporation was sold to the Dietrich family in 1927 and remained a privately held company until purchased by Hershey on October 27, 1986. Luden's introduced the *5th Avenue* candy bar in 1936.

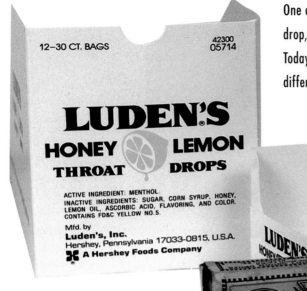

One of Luden's early and most famous inventions was the menthol amber cough drop, which is still among the best-selling products of its kind in the country. Today, as part of the Hershey Foods Corporation, Luden's produces several different kinds of throat drops and lozenges in a variety of flavors.

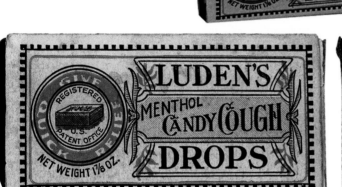

On August 28, 1986, Hershey Foods Corporation completed the purchase of Cadbury Schweppes' American confectionery operations in consideration of $270 million, plus the assumption of $30 million in debt. As part of the arrangement, Hershey was licensed to manufacture, market, and distribute Cadbury's brands in the domestic market, including *Peter Paul Mounds*, *Peter Paul Almond Joy*, *York* peppermint pattie, as well as *Cadbury's* label items, including *Dairy Milk*, *Fruit and Nut*, *Caramello*, and *Crème Eggs*.

One of Hershey's successful non-chocolate confectionery products, *Amazin' Fruit* gummy bears were introduced in August 1992.

number of regional brand names. At the end of 1993, on the eve of the 100th anniversary of the founding of the Hershey Chocolate Company, Hershey Foods Corporation had become the leading producer of chocolate, confectionery, and dry pasta products in the United States, with a significant international presence in developing and established world markets.

A VARIETY OF NEW PRODUCTS AND ACQUISITIONS

The introduction of successful new products has been and remains the key to the future success of Hershey Foods Corporation. Since the reorganization of the Corporation in 1988, Hershey has continued to introduce a variety of new and diverse products. For example, in 1989 alone, Hershey introduced a variety of grocery and baking products, including *Hershey's* strawberry syrup, vanilla milk chips, premium milk chocolate chunks, unsweetened and semi-sweet premium baking bars, and European-style cocoa; *Symphony* milk chocolate and milk chocolate with almonds and toffee chips candy bars; and the first *Hershey's* chocolate bar flavor puddings. In the following year, Hershey introduced *Hershey's* genuine chocolate drink; the first *Hershey's Chocolate Shoppe* toppings; and *Hershey's Kisses with Almonds*. In 1992, Hershey introduced a new reformulated *Hershey's Special Dark* candy bar; *Luden's* berry assortment throat drops; a fat-free line of puddings called *Hershey's Free* chocolate bar flavor puddings; *Amazin' Fruit* gummy bears in original and tropical flavors; and *Hershey's Cookies 'n' Mint* candy bar. In 1993, Hershey introduced three new baking products, including *Hershey's* raspberry semi-sweet chocolate chips, *Hershey's Skor* English toffee bits, and *Hershey's* holiday candy-coated bits. With the retirement of Richard Zimmerman in 1993 and the promotion of Kenneth Wolfe to chairman of the board and chief executive officer and Joseph P. Viviano to president and chief operating officer, the

Corporation continued to add to its value by taking advantage of new, profitable growth opportunities. Nineteen ninety-four, the 100th year of *Hershey's* chocolate production, saw the introduction of *Reese's Nutrageous* candy bar; *Reese's* peanut butter puffs cereal; a variety of candy bar–flavored ice cream sprinkles; a variety of *Hershey's Nuggets* chocolates; and *Hershey's* hot cocoa collection.

In August 1994, Hershey Chocolate introduced *Hershey's Nuggets*—thick and rich bite-sized chunks of your favorite *Hershey's* products. A bite of chocolate "we can sink our teeth into."

A NEW CENTURY BEGINS

In 1995, Hershey began a second century of operation with the introduction of *Reese's* peanut butter ice cream cups; *Hershey's Great American Cafe* nondairy creamers; *Amazin' Fruit* drink boxes in three flavors, including *Kangadude* fruit punch, *Orangutan Man* orange, and *Later Alligator* grape; and *Hershey's Cookies 'n' Creme* candy bar. In December 1995, Hershey Foods acquired Henry Heide, Inc. Heide products included such nonchocolate confectionery items as *Jujyfruits* candy, *Wunderbeans* jellybeans, and *Heide* jujubes. This acquisition was followed by the purchase of the operating assets and trademarks of Leaf North America in December 1996. Leaf's well-known

(Left) This is a point-of-purchase retail display poster for *Hershey's Chocolate Shoppe* toppings, in hot fudge and double chocolate fudge, which were introduced nationally in April 1990.

(Right) *Hershey's* milk chocolate fudge topping was introduced in January 1952 and discontinued in 1968. The *Chocolate Shoppe* toppings are yet another example of an updated product reintroduction.

(Left) *Promotional Support Materials, Christmas 1987.*

(Below) The *Rally* bar was introduced by Hershey in January 1970 and discontinued in January 1979.

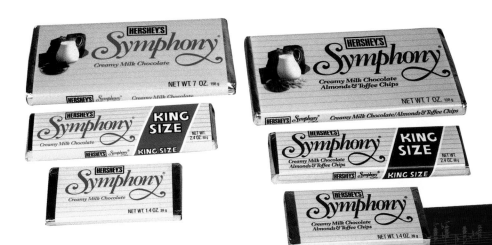

A creamier blend of milk chocolate, Hershey introduced *Symphony* in September 1989. It is a milder, more European flavor of milk chocolate.

Hershey's Chocolate World *Specialty Chocolates 1983–Present.* In addition to serving as an orientation area and information center for the public, visitors to *Hershey's Chocolate World* have been able to purchase specialty chocolates and other novelties at the facility since it first opened to the public on June 30, 1973.

chocolate and nonchocolate brands include *Good & Plenty* candy, *Heath* toffee bar, *Jolly Rancher* candy, *Milk Duds* chocolate-covered caramels, *PayDay* peanut caramel bar, and *Whoppers* malted milk balls. Nineteen ninety-six also saw the introduction of several new products under the *Hershey's* name, including *Hershey's Sweet Escapes* candy bars, the first line of reduced-fat chocolate confectionery products; *Hershey's TasteTations*, the first line of hard candies; and *Hershey's Pot of Gold* boxed chocolates, the first full-line entry into the boxed chocolate category in the United States and a leading boxed chocolate in Canada.

THE CORPORATION TODAY

Hershey Foods Corporation is the leading North American manufacturer of quality chocolate and nonchocolate confectionery and chocolate-related grocery products, as well as the leading North American producer of branded, dry pasta products. Hershey Foods also operates a variety of international operations in over 90 countries worldwide. The stated mission of the Corporation is to be a focused food company in North America and selected international markets and a leader in every aspect of business. In North America, the goal of the Corporation is to enhance its No. 1 position in both chocolate and nonchocolate confectionery and maintain its leadership position in pasta and chocolate-related grocery products. To achieve these goals, Hershey Foods Corporation is now divided into three operating divisions.

Hershey Chocolate North America encompasses operations in Canada, the United States, and Mexico. The division continues to produce and market many favorite American brands. Key American brands include *Almond Joy* and *Mounds* candy bars, *Cadbury's Crème Eggs* candy, *Hershey's Cookies 'n' Creme* candy bar, *Hershey's* milk chocolate and milk chocolate with almonds bars, *Hershey's Nuggets* chocolates, *Hershey's Kisses* and *Hershey's Hugs* chocolates, *Kit Kat* wafer bar, *Reese's Nutrageous* candy bar, *Reese's* peanut butter cups, *Sweet Escapes* candy bars, *York* peppermint patties, *TasteTations* candy, and *Twizzlers*. Additional brands include *Jolly Rancher*, *Jujyfruits* and *Milk Duds*

*Product Character, **Reese's** Peanut Butter Cup 1993. In 1973, Hershey introduced a new promotion featuring various product characters to greet visitors at the **Hershey's Chocolate World** visitors center and the **Hersheypark** entertainment complex.*

candies, *PayDay* peanut caramel bar, *Pot of Gold* boxed chocolates, *Whoppers* malted milk balls, and *Wunderbeans* jellybeans. Key Canadian brands include *Brown Cow* and *Strawberry Cow* milk modifiers, *Chipits* chocolate chips, *Eat-More* candy, *Glosette* candy, *Hershey* candy bars, *Oh Henry!* candy bars, *Pot of Gold* boxed chocolates, *Reese* peanut butter cups candy, and *Twizzlers* candy. In Mexico, chocolate products are produced and marketed under the *Hershey's* brand name. In addition, some of the division's products manufactured in the United States are sold in Mexico. In 1996, Hershey Chocolate North America was the leading confectionery company in North America. The division also continued to hold the leadership position in baking chips and sundae toppings in Canada, and held the No. 2 position in the expanded chocolate bar market in that country as well as the No. 2 position in the chocolate confectionery and flavored milk drink categories in Mexico.

Hershey Pasta and Grocery Group produces a broad array of dry pasta products under eight regional brands: *American Beauty*, *Ideal* by San Giorgio, *Light 'n Fluffy*, *P&R*, *Mrs. Weiss'*, *Ronzoni*, *San Giorgio*, and *Skinner*. Other grocery products include *Hershey's* and *Reese's* baking chips, *Hershey's* baking chocolate, *Hershey's* chocolate drink, *Hershey's* chocolate milk mix, *Hershey's Chocolate Shoppe* ice cream toppings, *Hershey's* cocoa, *Hershey's* syrup, *Hershey's* hot cocoa collection, and *Reese's* peanut butter. In 1996, the division continued to hold the No. 1 share position in the U.S. branded dry pasta category and the leadership position in the chocolate syrup and unsweetened cocoa categories in the United States.

Hershey International exports *Hershey's* branded confectionery and grocery products to over 90 countries worldwide. The division markets traditional *Hershey's* chocolate and grocery products, as well as *Hershey's Extra Creamy* milk chocolate, designed specifically to meet the preferences of international consumers. *Hershey's* branded products are also available through licensing agreements with partners in South Korea, Japan, the Philippines, and Taiwan. In Japan, *Hershey's Kisses* milk chocolates are the division's major confectionery product. The division continues to have a strong brand franchise in South Korea, where it is the recognized leader in chocolate beverages. One of Hershey's strongest markets outside of North America is the Philippines, where

*Product Character, **BarNone** Candy Bar 1993.* Hershey introduced *BarNone* in 1986. It was reformulated in 1993 to include caramel in addition to the original wafers, chocolate, and peanuts. This candy bar has since been discontinued.

Y&S Candies—An Integral Part of the **Hershey's** *Product Family.* Hershey Foods purchased Y&S Candies in 1977. Its largest plant is located in Lancaster, Pennsylvania. The Y&S trademark dates back to 1870 and stands for Young and Smylie. From 1902 through 1968, the company was known as the National Licorice Company. In 1968, it adopted the name Y&S Candies.

Hershey International. On July 6, 1981, Hershey Foods Corporation's international business interests were grouped into a new company, Hershey International, Ltd.

BarNone 1986–1992.

the division competes favorably in the domestic retail market and duty-free business. *Hershey's* chocolate products have been introduced in Russia and China and the division continues to pursue licensing and export programs worldwide.

A GREAT PLACE TO WORK

By any measure, Hershey Foods Corporation is recognized as a leading producer of chocolate, confectionery, and pasta products in the United States. The Corporation is also recognized as a superior place to work and has been included in the most recent edition of *The 100 Best Companies to Work for in America*, a book by Robert Levering and Milton Moskowitz. Levering and Moskowitz have conducted interviews with thousands of workers and managers throughout corporate America to determine the operations and "corporate culture" most rewarding to employees at all levels. The authors found Hershey Foods to compare quite favorably with other major American companies, especially in the areas of pay and benefits, advancement opportunities, job security, workplace pride, and employer openness and fairness. According to the authors, Hershey Foods is among the 100 best companies in offering a richer working environment and sharing a deep-seated respect for the people they employ.

Product Character, 5th Avenue Candy Bar 1993. The Luden's Candy Company introduced the 5th Avenue bar in 1936. Hershey acquired Luden's in 1986 and the rights to produce everything that was part of the Luden's product line, including 5th Avenue.

5th Avenue Candy Bar 1989.

A VISION FOR THE FUTURE

Today, even with the continued expansion and diversification Hershey Foods has experienced, it remains firmly committed to the vision of its founder and the welfare of its employees. Whether in good times or in bad, Hershey Foods employees have had the good fortune to work for a company that, like the man who founded it, judges its success by more than the money it earns. Milton Hershey's vision of a successful business, model community, and generous, continuing gift of opportunity to those less fortunate remains as meaningful today as it has for so many over the years.

Product Character, **Hershey's** *Syrup 1993.* Hershey's syrup in cans and squeeze bottles (which were initiated in February 1979) has been a mainstay of the product line.

The 24-ounce squeeze bottle as it looks today (left), and in 1979.

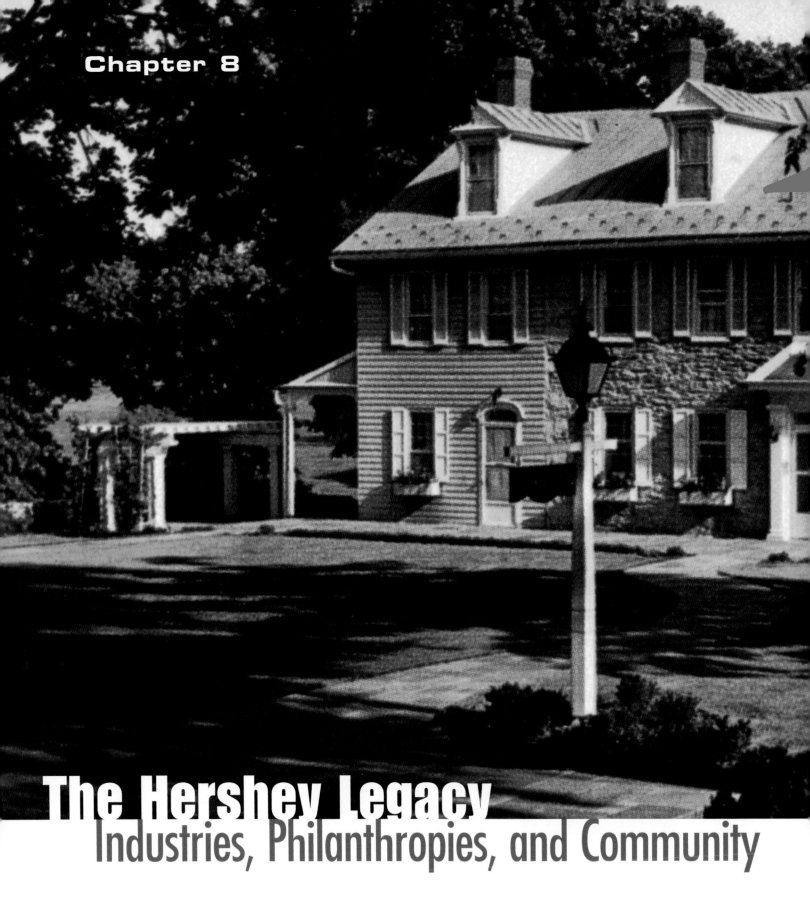

Chapter 8

The Hershey Legacy
Industries, Philanthropies, and Community

View of the Homestead, Milton Hershey School. Since August 1996, the Homestead has served as the campus headquarters for the Milton Hershey School's alumni activities. At the Homestead, the Hershey Room, where Milton S. Hershey was born, now serves as a memorabilia room. The school's three main educational buildings are Memorial Hall, completed in August 1995, which houses the Elementary School Program for children from prekindergarten through fifth grade; Catherine Hall, completed in 1966, which houses the Middle School Program for children in grades six through eight; and Senior Hall, completed in 1934, which houses the high school program.

The Hershey Museum of the M.S. Hershey Foundation. Milton Hershey created the Hershey Museum as a cultural and educational resource for his model town in 1933. Through engaging and lively exhibitions, programs, and other special events, the museum invites visitors to learn about the unique life of Milton Hershey and the many legacies he created and provided for.

During his own lifetime, the financial success of *Hershey's* chocolate provided Milton Hershey with the means to create a model community, a school for orphan boys, and facilities that met and served the public interest. In the years since his death in 1945, his legacy has grown and changed—but has never disappeared or been forgotten. The corporate legacy left by Milton Hershey is not all built on chocolate, confections, and pasta; the companies, industries, philanthropies, and town he founded continue to flourish.

HERSHEY ENTERTAINMENT & RESORT COMPANY

The corporate legacy left by Milton Hershey is not all chocolate, confections, and pasta. Many of the nonchocolate-producing businesses and commercial establishments originally grouped under the umbrella corporation known as Hershey Estates are still in existence today and have been joined by many others as well. In 1976, Hershey Estates was renamed Hershey Entertainment & Resort Company (HERCO). The company continues to be privately held as an asset of the Milton Hershey School Trust. Today HERCO owns and operates a number of hotels, sports and entertainment attractions, and commercial businesses, including *Hersheypark* Entertainment Complex, *Hersheypark* Arena/Stadium & The Star Pavilion, *ZooAmerica* North American Wildlife Park, *Hershey Bears* American League Hockey Club, *Hershey Wildcats* Professional Soccer Team, *The Hotel Hershey*, *The Hershey* Lodge & Convention Center, *Hershey* Highmeadow Campground, *Hershey* Nursery Landscape and Design, and *Hershey* Laundry & Textiles.

MILTON HERSHEY SCHOOL

As the living legacy of Milton and Catherine Hershey, the Milton Hershey School continues to provide a quality education and a nurturing residential environment for more than 1,100 students. The relationship among the school, Hershey Foods Corporation, HERCO, the Hershey Trust Company, and the community designed by Milton Hershey is believed to be unique in American corporate history and the continuance of this inter-dependent relationship has contributed to the fulfillment and protection of Hershey's philanthropic legacy. Milton Hershey School offers a complete prekindergarten through 12th grade educational and residential program to help students develop the sense of confidence and self-worth they need to have fulfilling lives through its three program levels: elementary, middle, and high school. The mission of the Milton Hershey School and School Trust, to nurture and educate financially and socially needy children in perpetuity, remains unchanged from Milton Hershey's original Deed of Trust.

Hershey Museum Exhibit Case. "Built on Chocolate" is the museum's principal permanent exhibit and pro-vides access to the many aspects of the Hershey story. This case contains many objects and graphics associated with the childhood of Milton Hershey.

THE M.S. HERSHEY FOUNDATION

Milton Hershey's interest in educa-tion extended beyond that offered to the children of the Milton Hershey School. In 1935, he created the M.S. Hershey Founda-tion to support academic education and cul-tural enrichment for any resident of Hershey and its municipality of Derry Township. Like the Milton Hershey School, its assets are also managed by the Hershey Trust Com-pany. The foundation originally supported the Derry Township Public School System and the Hershey Junior College. With the closing of the Junior College in 1965, the Foundation has shifted its focus to the cul-tural enrichment, entertainment, and edu-cation of the local community and the

The Hershey Gardens of the M.S. Hershey Foundation. Milton Hershey purchased "the boy with the leaking boot" statue pictured in the center of this image as an ornament for his private gardens in 1913. In 1936, Hershey asked his gardener to establish "a nice garden of roses" on three acres of land near *The Hotel Hershey.* Mr. Hershey was so pleased with the results that he increased the rose displays and added other flowering displays as well. Today, the Hershey Gardens covers 23 acres and includes major seasonal displays and botanical specimens. This statue still graces the central lake of the Hershey Gardens.

preservation of Milton Hershey's unique legacy. Through its four operating divisions—the Hershey Museum, the Hershey Community Archives, the Hershey Gardens, and the Hershey Theatre—as well as its ownership of *Chocolatetown Square* in downtown Hershey where a varied menu of programming for the community and visitors is offered during the summer months, the foundation supports a well-rounded "Hershey Experience" for over 20,000 Hershey residents and 2 million visitors each year. Through its classes, public programs and school services, performing arts productions, museum exhibitions, archival services, and formal garden displays, the M.S. Hershey Foundation plays an increasingly vital role in the financial and cultural well-being of its community.

THE MILTON S. HERSHEY MEDICAL CENTER OF THE PENNSYLVANIA STATE UNIVERSITY

Although it did not exist during Milton Hershey's own lifetime, the Milton S. Hershey Medical Center owes its existence to his generosity. In 1963, the Milton Hershey School Trust, through the M.S. Hershey Foundation, contributed $50 million and land to the Pennsylvania State University to help found the Milton S. Hershey Medical Center, comprising the Penn State College of Medicine, University Hospital, and Children's Hospital. Since its inception, the College of Medicine has educated more than 1,900 medical students and 3,000 nursing students who, as physicians and nurses, annually treat more than 10 million patients throughout the country. Last year alone, University Hospital admitted well over 17,000 patients and accommodated some 241,000 patient visits. As of July 1, 1997, the medical services of the Hershey Medical

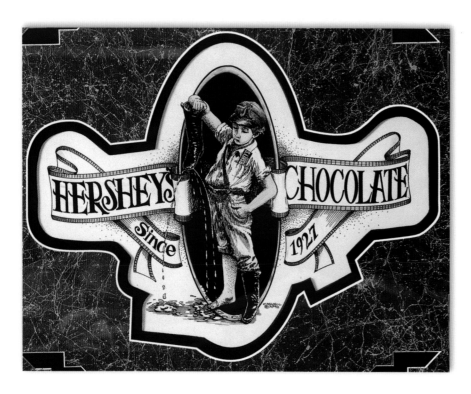

Center have been combined with those of the Geisinger Medical Center of Danville, Pennsylvania, to form the largest health care system in central Pennsylvania.

HERSHEY, PENNSYLVANIA

The people who are fortunate enough to call Hershey their home, who live and work in its environs, who are educated in its schools, or who just visit on a warm summer's day are the true recipients of Milton Hershey's generosity and living embodiments of his legacy. From the beginning, sound bites, slogans, and catchy phrases from "A Model Town" and "A Town to Meet Every Need" to the more recent "Chocolate Town, U.S.A.!" and "The Sweetest Place on Earth" have been used to describe and to entice visitors to Hershey. The town came of age during the years of the Great Depression when massive building projects personally selected and constructed by Milton Hershey came to be. A description of the town and its facilities from a *Hotel Hershey* promotional brochure from the late 1930s describes it best:

Souvenir Map Poster and Guide

Hershey—Chocolate Town, U.S.A.! Year-round excitement and world-class accommodations continue to make Hershey one of the premier vacation destinations in the northeast.

Mr. Hershey erected in 1933 a Community Building for the recreation and use of all the people. The structure, of Italian Renaissance design, modern in every respect, six stories high, covering six acres of floor space, houses the Community Theatre—as beautiful as any theatre in America—Little Theatre, Public Library, Dining Room, Cafeteria, Gymnasium, Swimming Pool, Game and Social Rooms, and Hospital.

Hershey has four golf courses of 54 holes, that have won for it the sobriquet of "The Golf Capital of America." Mr. Hershey, having a love for boys and girls and a keen interest in sports, built for the Juvenile Country Club—the only golf club in America exclusively for youth—a modern, rustic style club-house and a sporty 9-hole course.

For the recreation of people, 1,000 acres have been given over to *HersheyPark*, a place of clean, wholesome entertainment, which has

Christmas in Hershey. Although most people think of Hershey in terms of summer fun, the town of Hershey is busy with year-round activity. One of the largest townwide celebrations occurs each Christmas holiday season when the *Hersheypark* entertainment complex, *Hershey's Chocolate World* visitors center, and the Hershey Museum transform themselves into Christmas Candylane each holiday season. From mid-November through the end of the year, visitors, residents, and local businesses join together to provide a variety of entertainment for the entire family.

brought Hershey the title of "The Summer Capital of Pennsylvania." This park contains the usual summer park entertainment, a zoo covering 40 acres, the largest private zoo in the United States; the Hershey Museum; an outdoor series of swimming pools containing 1,500,000 gallons of filtered spring water; a ballroom where orchestras of national reputation play dance music; a clean picnic ground; band concerts in the outdoor bandshell; and the Sports Arena, seating 7,200 spectators for hockey, ice carnivals, roller skating, circuses, basketball and other sports. Immediately north is the *Hershey* Stadium.

In 1937 the Hershey Rose Garden, called "the most important rose garden in America," was opened to the public. It contains over 20,000 plants of more than 400 distinct varieties of roses of the world.

The community of Hershey also contains a Young Women's Club, with gymnasium and swimming pool; a Department Store, which sells anything the community needs; a Community Inn, a modern, moderate priced hotel; Hershey Trust Company and the Hershey National Bank.

The youth of Hershey and Derry Township are educated in the Derry Township Schools, the largest consolidated school system in

America, consisting of grade, junior–senior high and vocational schools. At the beginning of 1935, Mr. Hershey created the M.S. Hershey Foundation for the establishment and maintenance of one or more educational institutions and for the further education of girls and boys of Derry Township after they graduate from high school [a reference to the Hershey Junior College].

Even as the town of Hershey has continued to grow and to change, it has maintained its simple elegance and charm. One of the most eloquent (and admittedly most subjective) reviews of the benefits of the town and the place of Milton Hershey in the betterment of the human condition was also written in the late 1930s, this time by Hershey biographer, relative, and close friend, Joseph Richard Snavely. In describing his view of the Hershey legacy, Snavely wrote:

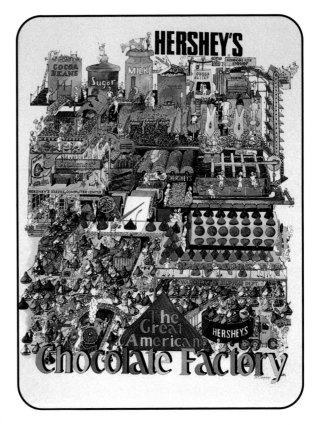

Hershey's—The Great American Chocolate Factory. Hershey-area artist Bruce Johnson did the cover of this souvenir tin for Hershey Foods. Fifty years after the death of Milton Hershey, the factory, town, and community remain living monuments to his foresight and vision.

Obviously the principal interest of Hershey is the chocolate industry, but the larger interest embraces the community that has grown around the industry. The high ideals and the staunch spirit of Hershey is expressed not in mere industrial gain but in community building in its relation to human values by providing opportunity to live sanely in right surroundings.

The meteoric eminence of the town is bewildering, even to those who were among its first citizens. In the material sense its progress has been almost unbelievable and yet the finer part is the spirit behind it.... The town gives to all the full benefit of the best. It combines the facilities and the advantages of the city with the perfect rural environment. It was built for fresh air and sunshine and equipped with every facility for sound education, social uplift and recreation.

Hershey is the crystallization of an ideal, the desire of its builder to found a model industrial community and to disprove the unpleasant contention that modern industry kills the souls of its workers. Hershey is

*The **Hershey Bears.*** Hershey's American Hockey League team has won several Calder Cup Trophies over the years, most recently in the 1996–97 season.

On September 13, 1995, the U.S. Postal Service issued a 32-cent postage stamp commemorating the philanthropic achievements of Milton S. Hershey. Over 5,000 attended the first-day-of-issue ceremonies held in the *Hersheypark* Arena. The Hershey Museum served as a first-day-of-issue stamp cancellation site. Designed for post office display, this poster is signed by the stamp's designer, Dennis Lyall, and hangs in the museum's "Built on Chocolate" display.

an example of a town that has influenced the industrial and civic atmosphere of the entire country. Because of it, other factories have been improved, and towns in which industrial employees live have been benefited. It has added much to the health, happiness, and prosperity of the nation.

And so we find that one man, with an indomitable will, and a plenitude of human kindness, has shown the world the possibilities of wealth in the attainment of that highly elusive phantom—Happiness. Truly to be able to create harmony out of the conflicting lives of thousands of men and women is a far greater art than the creation of a delicate symphony out of 1,000 discordant notes.

Mr. Hershey has gone far toward solving many of the problems of unrest that confront this nation today. Peace and prosperity reign in the beautiful valley in which he decided to cast his business lot, but this has not been what might be called a fortuitous happening. Imbued with high ideals, he dreamed and planned and built; and because he chose 'to put things first' a great success has been his reward.

Think of this man who in a few short years has built a beautiful town, forged on the anvil of good-will. Think of this man of many philanthropies who has planned that after his life-span is ended his good works shall not falter but shall go on unabated. It has been said that the only marks we make upon this world are contained in the records of what we do to benefit the world, to make it a better place because we have traveled through it."

Surely Milton S. Hershey has been one of those individuals.

Appendix
A SELECTED CHRONOLOGY

1826 / Homestead built by Isaac and Anna Hershey.

September 3, 1857 / Birth of Milton Hershey in the Homestead.

April 12, 1862 / Sarena Hershey, sister of Milton Hershey, born (dies 1867).

1872 / Milton Hershey apprenticed to Joseph Royer.

1876 / Milton Hershey establishes first business selling candy in Philadelphia.

1886 / After a series of business failures, Hershey establishes the highly successful Lancaster Caramel Company.

1893 / Hershey attends the Colombian Exposition in Chicago where he purchases German chocolate-making equipment.

February 8, 1894 / Lancaster Caramel Company incorporated with the Hershey Chocolate Company as a subsidiary producing baking chocolate, cocoa, sweet chocolate coatings, and novelties.

April 17, 1895 / *Hershey's* chocolate first sold commercially.

May 25, 1898 / Milton marries Catherine (Kitty) Sweeney in the rectory of St. Patrick's Cathedral, New York City.

February 1900 / *Hershey's* milk chocolate first sold commercially.

August 10, 1900 / Lancaster Caramel Company sold for $1 million. Hershey retains his chocolate-manufacturing equipment and the right to continue to manufacture chocolate using the *Hershey's* name.

March 2, 1903 / Ground broken for chocolate factory in Derry Church.

June 1905 / Factory completed. Chocolate-manufacturing machinery installed.

July 1, 1907 / Hershey begins manufacture of *Hershey's Kisses* chocolates.

May 25, 1915 / Introduction of *Hershey's* chewing gum (discontinued October 1, 1924).

August 9, 1921 / Introduction of mechanical *Kisses* wrapping machines and advent of trademarked plume.

November 20, 1925 / *Mr. Goodbar* chocolate bar introduced.

January 1, 1926 / *Hershey's* cocoa syrup introduced. Forerunner of *Hershey's* syrup, introduced for home use on April 15, 1928.

October 22, 1927 / Hershey Chocolate Corporation (the successor to the Hershey Chocolate Company) makes its initial public stock offering.

April 26, 1933 / *Mild and Mellow* bar introduced (discontinued December 29, 1941).

January 4, 1934 / *Not-So-Sweet* bar introduced (discontinued November 16, 1937).

October 3, 1934 / *Aero* chocolate bar introduced (discontinued May 15, 1939).

September 1937 / Initial development of *Field Ration D* bar.

November 1, 1937 / *Bitter-Sweet* bar introduced (discontinued February 1944).

September 14, 1938 / *Krackel* bar introduced.

November 14, 1938 / *Biscrisp* bar introduced (discontinued September 15, 1939).

June 12, 1940 / *Hershey's* hot chocolate introduced.

May 25, 1943 / *Tropical* chocolate bar introduced.

October 13, 1945 / Death of Milton Hershey.

1942–1948 / *Hershey's Kisses* chocolates not produced because of rationing of foil used in packaging.

June 24, 1954 / *Hershey-ets* candies introduced.

September 24, 1956 / *Hershey's* instant cocoa mix introduced.

February 2, 1959 / *Hershey's* mint chocolate introduced (discontinued February 1969).

September 14, 1959 / *Hershey's* vitamin-fortified syrup introduced.

October 8, 1959 / *Hershey's* chocolate-covered candy-coated almonds introduced.

February 5, 1962 / *Hershey's* sweet milk cocoa introduced.

November 27, 1962 / *Hershey's* Pennsylvania Dutch sweet chocolate introduced.

February 25, 1963 / *Hershey's* butter chip bar introduced (discontinued September 1968).

June 24, 1963 / Hershey Chocolate acquires the H.B. Reese Candy Co., Inc.

November 3, 1964 / *Handi-Bake*, a liquid baking product, introduced (discontinued February 1969).

March 23, 1965 / Chocolate Covered Candy Coated Peanuts introduced (discontinued December 1978).

March 9, 1966 / *Hershey's* Junior bar line introduced (includes milk chocolate, *Krackel*, *Hershey-ets*, and Chocolate Covered Candy Coated Peanuts packages).

February 19, 1968 / Hershey Chocolate Corporation changes its name to Hershey Foods Corporation. Chocolate manufacturing is organized under The Chocolate and Confectionery Division.

October 16, 1969 / Hershey Foods Corporation signs an agreement to begin marketing and manufacturing Rowntree MacKintosh products (*Kit Kat* and *Rolo*) in the United States.

November 24, 1969 / Five-cent milk chocolate bar discontinued. Ten-cent bar becomes the standard bar.

January 1970 / *Rally* bar introduced (discontinued January 1979).

October 18, 1971 / *Special Dark* bar introduced, replacing *Hershey's* semi-sweet bar.

December 12, 1973 / Hershey Foods Corporation adds nutritional labeling on its candy bars, a first in the confectionery industry.

January 1, 1974 / Fifteen-cent chocolate bar replaces 10-cent bar.

August 7, 1977 / The Chocolate and Confectionery Division of Hershey Foods is renamed the Hershey Chocolate Company.

September 2, 1977 / *Golden Almond* chocolate bar introduced.

September 7, 1978 / *Reese's Pieces* candies introduced.

December 8, 1978 / *Whatchamacallit* candy bar introduced.

January 1980 / *Big Block* bar introduced.

February 3, 1981 / *Skor* toffee bar introduced into two test markets.

May 23, 1983 / *Hershey's* chocolate milk (first premixed chocolate drink produced by Hershey) introduced.

March 1986 / *Grand Slam* candy bar introduced (discontinued September 1987).

September 1986 / *BarNone* candy bar introduced (reformulated 1993).

January 4, 1988 / Hershey Chocolate Company officially renamed Hershey Chocolate, USA.

August 25, 1988 / Hershey Foods Corporation acquires Cadbury Schweppes' U.S. confectionery operations, including the *Peter Paul Mounds* and *Almond Joy, York* peppermint pattie, and *Cadbury* brand names.

September 1, 1988 / *Hershey's* chocolate milk mix introduced.

September 26, 1989 / *Symphony* milk chocolate bars introduced.

April 1990 / *Hershey's Chocolate Shoppe* toppings introduced nationally.

September 18, 1990 / *Hershey's Kisses with Almonds* introduced nationally.

December 1990 / *Hershey's Desert Bars* delivered to the U.S. Army for Operation Desert Shield.

January 6, 1992 / *Reese's* peanut butter, in both smooth and crunchy versions, introduced nationally.

August 1992 / *Amazin' Fruit* gummy bears in original and tropical flavors introduced nationally.

November 1992 / *Hershey's Cookies 'n' Mint* bar introduced nationally.

March 1994 / *Reese's Nutrageous* candy bar introduced.

July 14, 1994 / *Hershey's Nuggets* introduced.

September 19, 1995 / *Hershey's Cookies 'n' Creme* candy bar introduced.

December 1, 1995 / Hershey Foods acquires Henry Heide, Inc.

1996 / Hershey Foods acquires Leaf, Inc.

Compiled from information supplied by Hershey Community Archives of the M.S. Hershey Foundation.

BIBLIOGRAPHY

"Built on Chocolate," exhibit script, Hershey Museum, 1992.

Castner, Charles Schuyler. *One of a Kind: Milton Snavely Hershey, 1857–1945.* The Kutztown Publishing Co., Inc., 1983.

Divone, Judene. *Chocolate Moulds: A History and Encyclopedia.* Oakton Hills Publications: Oakton, Virginia, 1987.

"Hershey Chronology," Hershey Community Archives, 1995.

"Hershey Foods Corporation Annual Report," 1996.

"Hershey, Pennsylvania: 50th Anniversary of Chocolate Town 1903–1953," Hershey, Pennsylvania: Hershey Estates, 1953.

"The Ingredients of Our Success," Hershey Foods Corporation 100th Anniversary, 1994.

An Intimate Story of Milton S. Hershey. Hershey, Pennsylvania: The Hershey Press, 1957.

Levering, Robert and Moskowitz, Milton. *The 100 Best Companies to Work for in America.* New York: The Penguin Books USA Inc., 1994.

"Meet Mr. Hershey," Hershey, Pennsylvania: The Hershey Press, 1939.

"Milton Hershey School Annual Report 1995–1996," 1996.

Milton S. Hershey, Builder. Hershey, Pennsylvania: The Hershey Press, 1934.

Morton, Marcia and Morton, Frederic. *Chocolate: An Illustrated History.* New York: Crown Publishers, Inc., 1986.

M.S. Hershey Lives On. Hershey, Pennsylvania: The Hershey Press, 1947.

Snavely, Joseph Richard. "A Chat with Mr. Hershey," Hershey, Pennsylvania: The Hershey Press, 1932.

Steinmetz, Richard H. "Chocolate Town Trolleys: An Illustrated History of the Electric Street Railway in Hershey, Pennsylvania," 1967.

"The Story of Hershey The Chocolate Town," Hershey, Pennsylvania: The Hershey Press, 1953.

"Views of Franklin and Marshall College, Lancaster, Pennsylvania," published in the interests of the College, 1906.

Wallace, Paul A. W. "Biography of M. S. Hershey," unpublished, 1955.

"Working at Hershey: A Handbook and Guide for the Men and Women at Hershey Chocolate Corporation," 1954.

RECOMMENDED READING

Ammon, Richard. *The Kids' Book of Chocolate.* New York: Macmillan Publishing Company, 1987. Children will enjoy reading the various facts in this book

Boynton, Sandra. *Chocolate: The Consuming Passion.* New York: Workman Publishing, 1982. Humorous book for chocolate lovers by the famed cartoonist

Broekel, Ray. *The Chocolate Chronicles.* Lombard, Illinois: Wallace-Homestead Book Co., 1985. A photo-filled history of the chocolate industry in the United States

Broekel, Ray. *The Great American Candy Bar Book.* Boston: Houghton Mifflin Co., 1982. History and unusual facts about past and present candy bars in America

Burford, Betty. *Chocolate by Hershey.* Minneapolis, Minnesota: Carolrhoda Books, Inc., 1994. Concise, easy-to-read story of Milton Hershey's life

Cassidy, Pamela and Harrison, Eliza Cope. *One Man's Vision: Hershey, A Model Town.* Hershey, Pennsylvania, 1988. Historic photos and factual account of Milton Hershey's successful town

Coe, Sophie D. and Coe, Michael D. *The True History of Chocolate.* New York: Thames and Hudson, 1996. A comprehensive history of chocolate in Europe and America

Foster, Nelson and Cordell, Linda S., editors. *Chilies to Chocolate: Food the America's Gave the World.* Tucson, Arizona: University of Arizona Press, 1992. Essays on various chocolate-related topics

Gregory, O. B. *Cocoa and Chocolate.* Windermere, Florida: Rourke Publications, Inc., 1981. Easy-to-read information

Jacques, Charles J., Jr. *Hersheypark: The Sweetness of Success.* Jefferson, Ohio: Amusement Park Journal, 1997. An in-depth look at the history of the world-class amusement park

Malone, Mary. *Milton Hershey: Chocolate King.* Champaign, Illinois: Garrard Publishing Company, 1971. Biography of Milton Hershey, middle elementary level

Milton Hershey: The Chocolate King. A & E Television Network. New York: New Video Group, 1995. 50-minute video on Milton Hershey produced for A & E's *Biography*

Mitgutsch, Ali. *From Cacao Bean to Chocolate.* Minneapolis, Minnesota: Carolrhoda Books, Inc., 1981. A picture book showing the sequence of how chocolate is made

Shippen, Katherine B. and Wallace, Paul A. W. "Milton S. Hershey." New York: Random House, 1959. A concise biography of Milton and Catherine Hershey

Index

Page ranges in italics include illustrations.